STANLEY SPENCER

A SORT OF HEAVEN

ISBN 1 85437-096-0

Published by order of the Trustees 1992
for the collection display, 25 March 1992 – 7 January 1993

Published by Tate Gallery Liverpool, Albert Dock, Liverpool L3 4BB
Edited by Judith Nesbitt
Assisted by Jemima Pyne and Helen Ruscoe
Designed by Jeremy Greenwood, Woodbridge
Printed in Great Britain by Balding+Mansell plc, Wisbech

Extracts from Spencer's writings in the Tate Archive are published with the kind
permission of The Stanley Spencer Estate

Photo credits
All works © Estate of Stanley Spencer 1992 All rights reserved DACS
Tate Gallery Photographic Department for all the works in Tate collection
The Imperial War Museum, London p32
Private Collection p14
The Syndics of the Fitzwilliam Museum, Cambridge p44
Stanley Spencer Gallery, Cookham, Berkshire p34
Williamson Art Gallery & Museum, Birkenhead, Wirral p28
Ivor Braka Limited, London p22
Private Collection, Liverpool p42

cover
The Centurion's Servant 1914 (p30)
frontispiece
*Notebook drawing: Stanley emerging from
a tomb* Tate Gallery Archive 733.3.19
(not in display)

CONTENTS

Sponsored by

MERSEYSIDE
DEVELOPMENT CORPORATION

PREFACE

From 1927, when his eighteen feet long canvas, 'The Resurrection, Cookham', was first shown, to critical acclaim, at the Goupil Gallery, London, Stanley Spencer has held a prominent and sometimes controversial position in British art. In many respects he is the antithesis of Walter Sickert, who has been the subject of a comparable display at Tate Gallery Liverpool. If Sickert represents the cosmopolitan face of British art, integrated to a European avant-garde, Spencer is identified with the Berkshire village of Cookham, his birthplace and home. But 'Cookham' does not explain Spencer, any more than Camden Town does Sickert. And as an ambitious young artist, Spencer was neither unaware of, nor unaffected by his contemporaries in the art world in which he sought recognition. Yet if these external influences were further catalogued, as they could be, it would still leave much unsaid. The heart of his work is to be found, described in its complexity, only in the artist's own words.

The Tate Gallery is fortunate to have, in addition to its outstanding collection of paintings and drawings by Spencer, an extensive archive acquired from the artist's family. These papers greatly illuminate the study of his work, and a small selection of the material is included in the present display. In these notebooks, letters and loose scraps of paper, Spencer made for his pictures, 'a special home. A place in my writings made for them'. The extracts published here are but a sample of this rich resource.

The Tate Gallery's holdings, though not comprehensive, are representative of the range of work which Spencer produced, and include several of his great pre-war pictures, his religious narratives, portraits, landscapes and drawings. This allows the visitor to make comparative judgements, as in fact Spencer did, between (to take just one example) the landscape passage in 'The Resurrection, Cookham' and his 'Pigs' landscape. We are delighted to be able to show 'The Resurrection, Cookham' for the first time outside London, in company with some distinguished loans, which augment the Tate Gallery holdings, without attempting to cover every aspect of his large and varied output. The Stanley Spencer Gallery, in Cookham, which this year celebrates its 30th anniversary, is among those who have lent to our display. We thank those, from private and public collections, who have generously given their support. It affords us all an opportunity to survey 'the infiniteness and possibility' of the world viewed through Spencer's mind's eye.

Nicholas Serota
Director, Tate Gallery

Lewis Biggs
Curator, Tate Gallery Liverpool   5

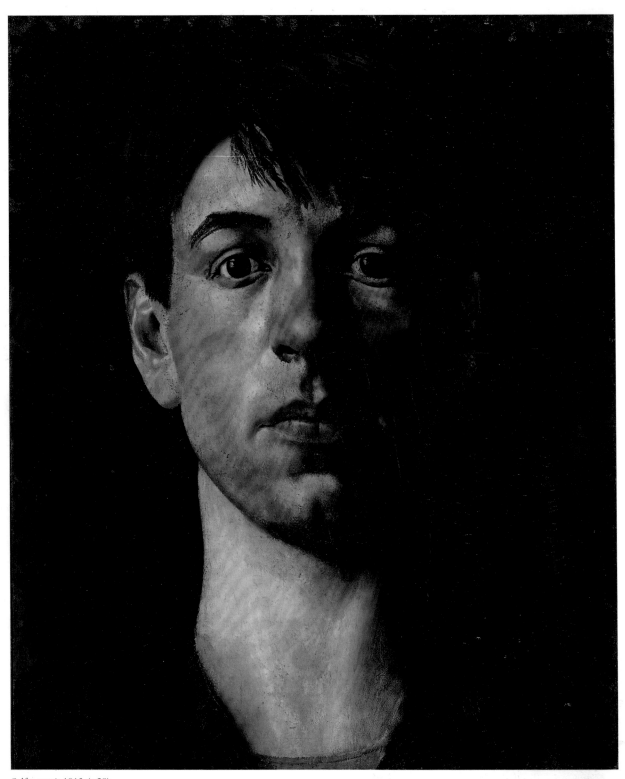

Self-portrait 1913 (p28)

COOKHAM'S PRESENT

Antony Gormley

Through the vicissitudes of the contemporary debate on Art Spencer persists – the man who painted because he couldn't do anything else, the man with the constantly flowing inner dialogue who never stopped looking and recording the twin views of the world around and the world within. He was inspired – or afflicted, whatever you will.

The years of Spencer's active life as an artist span the emergence of the Modernist trajectory from Cubism in France to Field Painting in the United States of America. Spencer made no contribution to this: he had other things on his mind. Histories have often been constructed to justify the present, implying that the present is better. Today we may usefully question the history of 'ever better methods' that has been applied to art. Spencer's work implicitly criticises the view that human development is allied to technology – and implies that such a view promotes *distance*. He projects an idea of life as *immersion* and the development of human consciousness as its purpose.

For Spencer love is a transforming power that is expressed most fully in human beings. Love is the real subject of art. Love is the force that both connects and redeems. It is the force that emanates towards things and joins them together. Spencer's gift and his gift to us in his art is this integrating power which starts with individual experience and reaches out to embrace what surrounds it locally and is at the same time connected to a wider world. Spencer insists on the mutual dependency of the real and the imagined world and he insists that art is a redemptive activity which can take the rejected or the ordinary and use it as the raw material of revelation. It is an art of affection undistanced by historical perspective and self-imposed stylistic prescriptions. His commitment to the personal and the parish is a celebration of the provincial as the necessary texture of the global and the root of language.

Spencer's position is radical. If the modernist trajectory was concerned with the development of perceptual language that, in order to be 'objective' and finally sublime, ended up by being anonymous, he stands for the absolute subjectivity of the artist – as a point of view (recorder) and point of experience (receiver of inspiration). If Modernism could be characterised as an emptying out in order to expose the viewer to a subjective experience of objective phenomena, Spencer believes in inclusiveness and the celebration of his subjective experience.

For me Spencer *is* the 1913 self-portrait – at one and a half times life size it has the intimate yet epic quality of his best work – so like Palmer or Dürer, looking at himself as his world, his material – this oil rich painting (the paint would soon dry out) of a boy absorbed in looking and yet self-absorbed – as if creating the world and being created at the same time: a boy filled with God, his chin prominent and slightly raised, a boy filled with possibility and faith in Art and himself.

I had thought for instance that the S.s with
whom I was then staying had understood
my big paintings but not a bit of it. M.rs
said of my "Zacharias" "I would like to
"have just the landscape part minus the
"figures". I agree that ~~that~~ I don't
seem able to manage these 'big figure'
pictures: that I can't seem to visualize
everything to the same degree of realization
Perhaps if I make a diagramme showing
why there is this failure of vision making
one part of my work to be done in a
different way & with a different sort of
vision from another, it might help to
explain

A B

Human feelings
about people
not fused but isolated
from the landscape part

Exterior landscape completely
assimilable to my mind. No trans-
mings required.

ALL
Fused.

ALL things
completely
fused.

Human sufferings which
readily assimilable. these
need to under go some changes...
the changes ...

Notebook drawing: diagram showing Spencer's 'internal' and 'external' vision Tate Gallery Archive 733.2.370 (not in display)

UNINHABITED HEAVENS

Judith Nesbitt

Spencer is a remarkable artist, both for his considerable achievement and his self-acknowledged failure. Page after page of his extraordinary writings address the gap between his aspiration and frustration, and any overview of his work will reveal the same. The discrepancy may initially be seen within the range of his work, in the diversity of subject and treatment between the charmed pre-war works, the religious scenes of the thirties, the 'sex pictures' of the twenties, the portraits and landscapes, and the later figure pictures. Just as he compulsively listed and numbered his paintings, so he classified the different kinds of work which he produced at various stages in his career. In his copious and self-critical notebook entries, Spencer reveals with the utmost candour, how as an artist he often felt hostage to the personal circumstances which dictated the kind of work he could do. He was keenly aware that some of his paintings were liked more than others, and he himself expressed strong and sometimes contradictory opinions on them. Much of his effort in writing is spent in attempting to bring coherence to an oeuvre which appears to lack it. The passages quoted here, and in the section devoted to them, reveal the wider framework within which he viewed his achievement, and allow us to assess how far his paintings hold together within his vision.

He was a harsh critic of his own and other people's work. In notes headed 'My feelings about Anna Karenina', Spencer wrote: 'Tolstoy does not . . . understand his job quite', making the charge that 'it's all compiling and weaving, not a concept as far as I can see. It may be that a very part of one's vision is the practical ordering and marshalling of material. But if that is so one must feel it as you read it – I didn't' [733.2.370*]. The 'pointless jumps' in Tolstoy's great work of fiction convinced Spencer that in it, 'the concept is absent'. He often imagined his own life's work in the form of a book, spurred by his determination to write his autobiography. This allowed him the opportunity to order his different activities into 'chapters', and to consider how one chapter related to another. 'I might describe how different things take me. How landscape takes me, how painting religious pictures does, how ship building pictures touch me and how falling in love and then desire etc takes me, and each something would be seen to be making points that belongeth to one whole' [733.2.287]. He admired the Italian master, Botticelli, for 'the utter oneness' of his work. 'Everything says Botticelli with the same degree of robustness, certitude and clarity', he noted. Michelangelo, on the other hand, did not achieve this degree of integrity: 'I feel there are bits of Michelangelo wandering about here and there and not knowing what they are there for . . . one feels he is unaware of bits of debris and stuff that is him that we see and he doesn't' [733.2.10]. It is an open question as to which of the two artists Spencer most resembled. If he hoped for 'utter oneness', he himself acknowledged that often his reach exceeded his grasp.

Spencer's 'vision' was 'to do what isn't done, to supply what oneself alone can supply' [733.2.9]. So involved and complex was this process that he resorted to diagrams to explain the circumstances both when it worked, with 'all things completely fused' between his internal and external perception, and when things did not fuse, remaining isolated and 'not readily assimilable' [733.2.370]. More poetically, he described the inspiration of his early pictures as coming from 'a sort of internal prayer and fasting; it comes from a miracle of nothing or seeming nothing, it is a moving upon the face of the waters of one's own hope'.

The 1914–18 war was the first disruption of his precarious vision which he had begun to realise in the two years after he left the Slade School. 'From the time I left Cookham for the 1914 war and until I married in 1925 my life ceased to be a part of my work and conscious being. I went into my shell and took with me mentally all I could. So that with the exception of one or two occasional observations as an aid to assist me in remembering being something,

* Tate Gallery Archive reference number

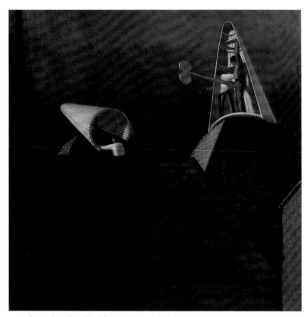

Mending Cowls, Cookham 1914 (p30)

I took little note, in any vital sense, of what went on. So that although I managed up to a point with Hilda, I never have succeeded to establish real contact in life at all. My work has all only been an expression of an unrealised life, though not an unreal one' [733.2.128]. The last distinction is telling: to Spencer something could be real, but remain unrealised. When his personal 'interior' life failed to activate his work, its absence gave 'a certain off-the-top film-like lifeless feeling to most of the work I then did' [733.2.128]. This vivid description perhaps best fits his landscapes, which he pronounced 'dead, dead'. He wrote at length about them, teasing himself that he did so as a form of confession. He outlined several reasons for doing them: to emulate his brother Gilbert (whose success in landscape painting he envied), to occupy him when he felt unable to do anything else, and, not least, to earn money. It was a bitter irony that the works he least valued were his most popular and saleable. Part of his resentment with landscape was his failure to realise an imaginative transformation of his subject, as he felt his brother achieved. Thus, on one landscape painting expedition with Gilbert and Henry Lamb in Dorset, he struggled till after dusk with a composition, earning the humiliating taunt from Lamb that next time he should bring a lantern. Of this difficulty, Spencer observed: 'my imagination never works faced with

objects or landscape'.

Writing an early monograph on Spencer (in The Penguin Modern Painters series in 1947) Eric Newton made a clear distinction between his imaginative works and those 'purely documentary statements of fact in which the physical eye alone has been consulted – the landscapes, most of the portraits, the studies of flowers and still lifes – pictures that are sometimes quite aggressively unimaginative, as though the artist had tried to turn himself into a camera' (Newton, Harmondsworth, 1947, p7). The analogy is the artist's own: 'In all of those landscapes I have more or less only been a camera: a camera that had some inkling of what I liked, and which arranged everything in about the point of view and angle I should want when I want to consider the next stage, namely a figure painting . . . I selected those places to do from the point of view of being places I liked to imagine people being in, those people being my own particular brand of people that I like' [733.2.87]. Places to Spencer were 'uninhabited heavens' and the loneliness he describes in standing, like a post, painting landscapes, is communicated in the best of them, which have a chilling air of abandon.

In another revealing analogy, the artist compared his landscapes to being like 'women I have failed to marry. Something has only been indicated and not consummated in them' [733.2.87]. His need to love and possess the subject relates the landscapes to the portraits, particularly his nude portraits. It is the unconsummated nature of his relationship with Patricia Preece (his second wife) which is the real drama of the startling double nude portraits (pp44 and 45). Only when the living subject became 'so much a part of that inner reality as to seem to become, because now so personal, hardly credible as an external thing' could his vision be realised [733.2.422]. Patricia remained resolutely credible, outside his vision. If, as in these portraits, the subject resisted his imaginative possession, it left him spiritually unengaged and isolated.

It was not only his landscapes which let him down. Some of his sex pictures of the thirties, the 'couples' and 'adoration of girls' series, done in compensation for his enforced celibacy, were to his mind 'never consummated'. This did not stop him regarding them with admiration and affection, on a par with his spiritually inclined works: 'I could take some of my sexual pictures and transpose them to religious ones and no-one would know' [733.3.22]. So uncompromising were his judgements that there was a degree of dissatisfaction with even his greatest pictures, as his accounts of 'The Centurion's Servant' (p30), 'Swan Upping at Cookham' (p13) and 'The Resurrection, Cookham' (p40 and 41) demonstrate. He even mocked his beloved 'Zacharias and Elizabeth' picture (p14) as just 'a vamped up piece of cooking', stung no doubt by the *Observer* art critic's jibe that in Spencer's picture, Zacharias wears a chef's hat. But elsewhere he affirmed its particular importance: 'Nothing other than complacence could produce another Zacharias'. It was complacence which he feared most of all, and this he felt produced his landscapes. Nonetheless, he did not disown them, listing them, and classifying them, according to their 'feeling and emotion', some as 'religious', some 'domestic', others 'romantic', making note of those he thought the best. Clearly some were less unrealised than others.

If, on occasion, Spencer 'forsook the vision' or the vision forsook him, he still hoped to see all his works as partaking in the unity he sought for. His Church-House scheme was intended to bring together not only his religious and sex pictures – the two main paths in his imaginative life – but all his other subjects. A room of his nude portraits 'would show how much they balance the need and the whole cosmical conception. There might also be a garden room, an object room and a landscape room' [733.8.2]. So varied was his scheme that there would even be 'a room of cattle in the field and a room of heads'.

Spencer loved the idea of diversity within unity. He relished the 'wonderful difference' beween one part of Cookham and another, affirming that 'it was all Heaven for that matter'. He wrote, similarly, of how a room asserts its particular atmosphere independent of its physical position in the house, just as the members of his house were one family but individual. This belief extended to his pictures, which could all be seen to belong together, and to belong to him: 'I have noticed that in all my various desires that they *have* a relationship to each other that there is a consistent something in all of them and that at different periods of my life they or many of them

Turk's Boatyard, Cookham c1931 (p43)

come together and suggest some clue as to what their final form is. This final form, the thing that the ecstasy is about: God can alone give the order and reveal their design'. If all Spencer's works do not say Spencer 'with the same degree of robustness, certitude and clarity', it was not for the want of a vision.

NOTEBOOKS

edited by Judith Nesbitt

The following extracts are selected from the extensive archive of Spencer's writings, acquired for the National Collection from his family. The majority are taken from his many notebooks, written in pencil. In his urgency, sometimes he used just loose scraps of paper, but Spencer named and numbered these notebooks, and all of them are well thumbed from his constant re-reading. Since much of it was written for his planned autobiography, he intended that the writings should illuminate his life and work and show the connection between them. Some are in the nature of diary entries, personal and introspective. He wrote most in the late thirties and forties, at a time when personal circumstances may have made his self-assessment give way to self-doubt. This being so, the tenacity of his vision is all the more remarkable. Spencer's exacting thought process involved many shifting critical judgements on his work, which can be seen even in this small sample. There are passages of luminous thought and expression, and some are more argumentative and 'rollicking'.

The autobiography never came to fruition, and so what remains is effectively his first draft – scarcely punctuated, with highly original spelling. These excerpts have been reproduced with only minimal correction of spelling and punctuation for clarity.

733 numbers refer to Tate Gallery Archive.

733.2.10 notebook entry headed 'Life drawing and Composition', in which Spencer reflects on his student training at the Slade School, and his transition to a more personal artistic idiom. Compares Botticelli's 'utter oneness' of meaning and expression to the 'whirlwind' of Michelangelo.

While as soon as I began to study drawing at the Slade I could feel myself developing in some sort of way, towards being able to draw, and could feel also that this would enable me to cope with the matter I had to express, yet nonetheless I did not study with any degree of intelligence, and the result of this was that I noticed that when any of this ability showed itself it had nothing to do with what I was trying to express. It was simply some object or place drawn in a way that showed this particular species of ability; a thing which had no connection with the thing drawn. They were not a perfect marriage between artistic capacity and special personal feeling. To express what I felt in Cookham with the particular kind of capacity I developed at the Slade might have been utterly and idiotically wrong. My knowledge developed by the experience of a series of drunken experiences, one not being in any way related to the other. It was only by a fortunate accident of circumstances that I found that here and there the quality I sought for in my drawing had a sort of twin relationship or fellow feeling for some feeling I had for some situation I wanted for a picture. I hoped in a very unintelligent way when at the Slade that perhaps what I learnt there might 'come in handy' some day.

I notice often in an artist's work that the *method* of expression has not the same unique character as the essential meaning of the picture. The good picture is when the way (ie the particular character of sensibility evinced in the carrying out) is inseparable from the essential meaning and beauty of the picture. This utter oneness is very marked in Botticelli: looked at from every viewpoint and in every mode and way the picture is expressed each way is contributing to the integrity of the whole. Everything says Botticelli with the same degree of robustness, certitude and clarity. This utter fusion of all the amazingly varied feelings and sensibilities that must have been in an artist of his calibre into one pure creative product Botticelli. Michaelangelo does not achieve the same degree of integrity and fusion, here and there you can see the parts that go to make the whole. There are less essentially Michaelangelo qualities mixed with essential qualities. I feel there are bits of Michaelangelo wandering about here and there not *quite* knowing what they are up to or what they are there for. His queer character comes surging towards us buoyed almost drunkenly on the gigantic stream of his feeling. We are at liberty to gaze upon all there is of him to see as he whirls past but one feels he is unaware of bits of debris and stuff that is him that we see and he doesn't. He seems to be not completely in control. He has to 'let it come'.

733.2.44 in which Spencer describes the complex evolution of one picture 'Swan Upping at Cookham' (right), and his fondness for it, when he longed to return from the war to complete it.

The thought in my mind of going on the river was somewhat different from the actual experience. If I was for instance in a pew in the church just behind this scene in the picture and it was while the 11 o'clock Sunday morning service was proceeding, my mind would be thinking of many things and the effect of being in church would be affecting my thought so that all my thoughts and feelings were a little different from what they were when outside. I liked projecting these thoughts produced in this atmosphere which as I say were of a special brand, beyond the church walls and out of first one and then another church window, back into the village or down to the river. When I did so I noticed that the village seemed as much a part of the atmosphere prevalent in the church as the most holy part of the church such as the altar. And so I felt that just as the atmosphere, as the altar was approached, became more tense and holy so the increase of atmosphere would further increase if one could get through the wall or through the pictures in the glass windows to the world beyond it. And so when I thought of people going on the river at that moment my mind's imagination of it seemed as I say to be an extension of the church atmosphere. When afterwards I looked at these places I had been thinking about in church, or rather first drew some idea of the place in the attic at home and then had a look at the actual place I noticed that there was indeed a signification in the place which was exactly the place in my mind. This meant that the place itself immediately became the special part of my mind which was to be the abode for all I wished to put in it. It meant this that I could now take any of these thoughts and put them where I felt they should be, with the confidence and assurance I needed. The people become because of the intense union I see between them and the place, a part of or permanent parts of the place. With this home to go to, this place in reality for my thoughts to live in, they became stranger and more robust until they were able to stroll out of my mind down to the boathouse and river and became the activities you see taking place there,

Swan Upping at Cookham 1914–19 (p31)

not only without losing the identity they had in my mind as being parts of me but finding greater being and significance through their having got into the plain daylight of the riverside.

As to the picture as a painting there is one circumstance which seriously interfered with the painting of it. The whole of my experience in the nearly four years of my being in the 1914–18 war comes between the painting of the upper and lower half of this picture. As the war drew to an end it became agonizing to me wondering if I should be snatched away. Apart from greed for life I felt I had got a lot up my sleeve that I wanted to produce before I died, and every day I was being detailed off for worse and worse dangers. As an infantry man what would have been the use of this insignificant fragment of gun fodder that I was if I had said to the sergeants 'I have a picture at home and I just want to finish it before going into this attack'. In any case I was in the Vardar Valley preparing for a big offensive while my picture as I hoped was where I left it at home in Cookham. It was just the fact that there was a remote possibility that I might still be living in a time of peace and no war and painting this picture up in my bedroom at home that was so agonizing. I was optimistic   13 also and seemed to see in all that looked peaceful something which suggested that peace was near, that we were on the edge of it. This made the sudden appearance of fresh supplies of ammunition arriving and orders for the beginning of a new offensive insupportable to the spirit. It can be imagined what I felt when I did at last in fact walk into my bedroom at home and see this picture leaning with its face to the wall on the far side of the big bed. I walked round the bed to it and laid my hands on it once more. Well there we were looking at each other; it seemed unbelievable that it was a fact. Then I wondered if what I had just come from was fact and caught sight of the yellow of the liddite or whatever the Bulgars used in their shells on my fingers and fingernails. It was a very difficult matter getting back to this painting. Here and there one would hardly notice any change of way of painting as for instance in the lower and upper portions of the punt cushion, but the river which I was doing so well as I think is nothing like so good in the nearer part of the picture. Oh no it is not proper or sensible to expect to paint after such experiences.

Zacharias and Elizabeth 1914 (p29)

733.3.22 dated December 1938, in which Spencer makes criticisms of 'Zacharias and Elizabeth' and 'The Resurrection, Cookham', and describes the relation between his 'sex' pictures and his religious pictures. Compares two examples of his landscape painting.

O that I could write only and solely of this moment in this room this afternoon. It would suit me if I felt able to never stir from just what I am feeling now. All that I have been and done before I came to live here, would be an intrusion. I love to contemplate the possibility of a theme being born out of the air of this room. A 'birth' of me taking place this afternoon in here. There have been many births of me, and this is one of them . . .

I approach those earlier times with a feeling of disinclination and having as much chance of once more experiencing those images as a harlot would have with a saint. There is only one thing that turns me in that direction and that is that all I did then was what conviction and faith in me such as it was, could produce . . .

In the picture called Zacharias ['Zacharias and Elizabeth' above] the chief figure in the foreground which is meant to be Zacharias making some sacrifice is the *only* weak thing in the picture and is the most important thing so that that picture is a very good shell and nothing in it or worse still contains a piece of vamped-up cooking. When I was doing it everything came clearly and fairly simply except that

figure and finally I merely 'inserted' a figure instead of leaving an empty space. Now I will come to the 'Tate' Resurrection ['The Resurrection, Cookham' p40 and 41]; what's all that under the porch? Once again everything was clear except the chiefest and most important thing and once again I was robbed of that special privilege of succeeding where success is vital and must be. No, all that in the porch is not in the concept; it would never come and finally had to be left to take its chance in the dangerous and dubious realm of after thought. And that is what it looks like and that is what it is and it isn't much at that. And what about 'Christ Carrying the Cross' (p35)? Where is Christ? and how unconvincing when you see him? All this failure . . . It might be then wondered why do pictures on such themes and the answer is that if I had not had that subject I could not have thought of *any* of that picture. In the religious realm I was never at any time able to discover one detail in the appearance of the chief religious figure in any picture of mine that in any way identified or disguised it and in every case where after years of waiting I have inserted a failure in the place of what should have completed and fulfilled the concept. Jesus was the trouble from my babyhood. I had hitched my chariot to that star and that star unfortunately for me was completely invisible. By which I mean that there was some to me vital association between what I felt I wished to express and this particular and prescribed Christ and Christian Doctrine element of religion . . . in order to perceive anything I had to enter and surround myself with the atmosphere of belief

14

and religion before I could get into that receptive mood, yet even so what I did perceive and draw expressively fell between two stools namely it was always evidently part of some concept the more important part of which was missing. Take for instance The Gardener in the Zacharias picture. I had decided on the Garden and on the subject and inspired by this I went to the little landing window and in the garden the Gardener was dragging along a bunch of ivy. [This] had only been deemed important by me in view of what I hoped the complete concept would be otherwise to me it would be nothing . . . Also there is the glaring fact staring me in the face, namely this, that when after twenty years and more of futile effort ending with the Tate Resurrection and the Burghclere Memorial, I at last could not stand the strain of this constipation, began to make a sexual urge the central theme, there and then, I saw that at least the central theme in each picture was emphatic if you like and the whole drama was complete. I saw also, and this last was what interested me most – that the religious quality I had been looking for and had never found in my work now for the first time showed itself. It is a bitter experience to me that this quality of feeling would never appear under that former religious sky where it could have meant everything to me and fulfilled much greater dramatic purpose, but only appear under this sky where it would hardly be recognised to be what it is and where what it could mean to me would again be limited through not including my own will in its making and consequently lacking in atmosphere and some sort of finality and dramatic import. These sex pictures stop short of something I need and which the pre-war pictures had. The only thing I complain of in the sexual avenue of development is that on the one hand I cannot get as far along that avenue as I feel I could along the other and also I am all the time being mastered instead of being the master . . . I have more to thank the sex road for than the other. I have very little to thank the deity for . . .

In spite of appearance I am convinced that these qualities are not the Devil's property and that they belong to the ordered and controlled avenue of my mind where they will do better work and I feeling more fulfilled would do them better. But I have done all them under his auspices and I must give the devil his due . . . I can see how my marriage experience from 1923 to the present day has affected my work. I had always found that every experience I had had some sort of effect on my work and I wished all experience to be an integral part of my work that was why I wished and hoped that my first marriage would form part of my religious outlook. But it did not . . . I was forever trying to force *that* experience into the religious one in my work and that is why my work became tainted and soon lost its fragrance. It was gone in one stroke and has never returned . . .

All I did (landscape excepted) was influenced and coloured by my domestic experience; whatever I missed in life found its way into my work . . . Painting is now a means for comforting myself for what I miss in experience and until and unless something is done to rehabilitate me so that my natural desires can be satisfied without the upsetting and disintegrating effect taking place that used to occur in my first marriage and the impotence I have found in myself in my present marriage so that I am obliged to live a celibate life, I shall, I know never be balanced in that way and my work will suffer . . . I am full of self pity and I need it, it will come from nowhere else . . .

But the continual breaking in of landscape work etc made [full revelation] not possible. In its final form: I know the nature of the state of peace in which I work when that part is reached and know that all I was trying to control belonged to that state and in that state would have been a very different matter to what they are now. . . . The only thing I wanted and never managed to get was some sort of comprehensive 'setting': a framework such as I found in the subject of the Resurrection which held me firmly while I viewed the world. I wanted to see all these things through eyes such as that subject gave me . . .

The relationship of the sex pictures to my religion is that they are like some incident happening in a religious picture: they are in the same world and atmosphere it is just that I can't get into the foreground part of those pictures where the religious happening and purport of the picture clear. They are *on their way* to a religious finality . . .

So often people imagine that to do a thing well needs only application and great care. I do my landscapes with a great deal of application and care, but they are dead, dead. They are done in the same spirit that I did company drill on the parade ground, that was also done with great care and application. I think a very striking example of how the forced and arbitrary elimination of the special spiritual quality of feeling that I need has affected the painting of for example landscape in my work can be seen by comparing the landscape part of my recent pigsty landscape with the landscape part of my Resurrection painting. They were both hanging next to each other when I went to the Tate the other day and I felt how lifeless the Pig landscape looked ['Rickett's Farm, Cookham Dene' p45]. And it is the case with all my landscapes. I am sure it is only I that have noticed this.

A concept is a work the whole of which in every detail and particular it is clear and undeniable has been dictated ordered and directed by God . . .

But there is one thing I will *not* do and that is to desert *both* of these spirits and dwell in the neutral land of landscape painting that I bloody well won't do and that is where I can see everyone trying to shove me and that is why they shall not see this. They are piqued to have to conclude that in liking these landscapes they have been shown up and are now trying to save their faces by making out these landscapes are better than my other works and have enough sense to tell me so. And now they have got to the point of trying to bully me into doing them using any and every pretext. Every form of coercion has been used 1. by making my landscape work a great financial success, and 2. by carefully refraining from buying any of my figure pictures. 3. by preaching to me in a 'fatherly' manner 4. by insulting and impudent behaviour.

733.3.33 in which Spencer considers why people prefer the 'landscape' parts to the figures in his paintings, and describes how he decides what subject to take.

If I conceive of two or more people in a picture I must be assured that there is no sexual barrier between them. In the whole or most religious enjoyment of nature there is no question of barriers; that is why it is enjoyed and possibly the *real* reason why many people like not to have 'figures' in a 'landscape'. They won't be had up for any degree of romantic and intimate association such as Wordsworth with trees and grass etc but if you want the same degree of association with human beings? I am often amused at the dislike people have of pictures of mine where the people have liked the 'landscape' part of it have disliked the figures as they coldly call them. And they have said that it wasn't because of any of the usual complaints about my 'figures' but because they wanted the landscape part to themselves in the same way as they want the countryside itself free for them to express and enjoy their own emotions in or the way they want a man or woman exclusively. The figures in my pictures where the landscape was pre-eminent were to those people an intrusion . . .

One has not only got to perceive the identity of a person or a bush, but the identity of the person and bush considered together, joined together to make some new identity, just as if an arm and a leg had been found and the finder was one who did not know of the existence of arms and legs joined to a body and could only therefore arrive at any further identification of their nature by approaching

nearer to essential harmony when through love and desire it might discover the further identifying factors of its nature in their both belong[ing] to one body . . .

In describing these further to my work ideas, it is noticeable that I am never preoccupied with *how* I paint but with the gradual development of my thought and affection towards life in general and from that to observing what in me it emotionally inspires me to do. There in that realm I know the strength that can be derived from knowing what I will do . . .

I have noticed in all my varied desires that they *have* a relationship to each other that there is a consistent something in all of them and that at different periods of my life they or many of them come together and suggest some clue as to what their final form is. This final something, the thing that the ecstasy is about: God, can alone give the order and reveal their design . . .

What I think about belongs to a theme; the life of the Buddha, the life of the Stanley, or the life of Christ, or all in me, certainly everything, God, Buddha, Christ, me or sticks of wood or thought of any kind that I had and liked would be included. I have always disliked the prejudice that exists between the religions. In a way the higgledy-piggledy order in which I see these things is the right order. Order of the conventional kind so often suggests precedent and in my all being equally great, equally God idea I would wish my heaven to be a kind of Jungle, but with all the people and animals on a love footing with each other . . .

In the matter of wishing to paint or a wish to paint something much in my case could be explained. The wish to paint came as a result of wishing to express something about something. Knowing *what* to paint in my case gives me the appetite for painting. If I simply take as a subject to paint, whether a particular place for a landscape or a figure picture, [it] is not necessary to consider whether it is 'suitable' for a landscape or figure picture, but whether I feel happy looking at it or thinking of it. I have to sound my emotional or spiritual feelings. I view the matter from the point of view of its turning into a lying in the direction of my own personal wishes, desires and beliefs. There is no looking to see if it makes a good composition; those are the things which, if I sound myself in this matter, will look after themselves.

733.2.87 headed 'Landscapes' in which Spencer provides a positive account of his landscape paintings, as 'preludes' to other pictures he might hope to do, categorising them according to their 'emotion'; describes the significance of place.

Although I am not pleased with myself over my landscape work it never having been what I intended or wanted to do and having done them only to get money, I am interested to note several things about them. In a great number of them they could be regarded as studies or preludes to a picture or pictures I might hope to do. There are those which have a definite emotion as their basis and on the strength of which the subject has been chosen. These landscapes containing some species of my own personal feeling and emotion group themselves roughly into four or five classes. Those which have attracted me by:
1. The special religious atmosphere they suggested
2. The Domestic and homely atmosphere
3. My own sensitiveness to shapes and forms and composition etc.
All these feelings of mine might be found in some measure, in each and any landscape of mine, but the grouping is meant to point to the dominating factors in them. Even in what I might consider as a fourth group namely the landscapes done in foreign countries, there is the domestic element in some of them.

I am aware that this may be not a bit why my landscapes are liked or what anyone likes them for. It is a temporary grouping I have made and which I feel to be so, in order that I can point out certain efforts that I continually make to bring all these feelings and desires together. Why I regret that they are still only landscapes is that being so they are as women I have failed to marry. Something has only been indicated and not consummated in them . . .

I will for the moment leave out the third and fourth groups in order to mention a fifth group that should in importance have been the third. It is a group in which the selection seems capable of sympathising with and absorbing I should think all my emotions. It contains strong elements of the Religious and Domestic needs but also a special atmosphere in which I find a peace that is not disturbed by having to absorb any of the varied desires I have. Perhaps for the sake of reference I will call it *Romantic*. But really it contains in equal parts well balanced most if not all my emotion. In this connection I can only think really of one landscape. It is called 'General View from Harwood House, Cookham Dene' (1938). In all my ceaseless efforts to cater for my own needs this landscape and one or two others came nearest to obliging me . . .

Terry's Lane, Cookham c1932 (p43)

But this last mentioned landscape group does add to my assurance that somewhere my different emotions do not clash, as now they sometimes do but meet and fuse and are one in peace. My varied emotions may, because of my weakness in not being able to decipher them, have become reactionary, but, I know that when I have arrived at a point of balance or equilibrium they will none of them either have to be deserted or very much change their natural (excepting to become more emphatic in their own several directions) to enable them to take their proper order and final resting place when once I have reached that place myself. I don't mind them; my emotions I mean; I mind whether I convert to the ends I wished them to serve. To look at the landscapes I have cited under the Religious heading; it seems as if the emotion is inseparable from Cookham, and to those who do not know how my religious emotions arose, a sort of wealthy riverside drawing-roomy atmosphere snobbish and pretentious seems to prevail. But to me as a child a grand house is sometimes a sort of Heaven and as a child I used to peep through chinks and cracks in fences etc and catch glimpses of these Gardens of Eden of which there was a profusion at Cookham. From these glimpses I used to get I assumed that some sort of saint or very wonderful person lived there and so on. If I was not so sure of that I invented and invited Biblical Characters to take over. That is what has taken place in the 'Zacharias and Elizabeth' painting (p14). Not that the people who owned that garden were at all unpleasant, on the contrary the owners of that Garden and house allowed me to go into it as often as I liked. In fact the residents' non-inclusion in that picture is more due to the fact that I never saw them there and the place seemed empty except for the gardener who was included in that picture, dragging along a branch of ivy which I saw him doing. There is a group of landscapes in which at least two of these chiefest emotions I have namely the Religious and

17

the Domestic elements equally predominate and which fuse . . .

In all these landscapes the thing I seek chiefly is to express a crucial meaning I find in its status as a place and what makes it *there* and nowhere else. I do so I think because a place is somewhere one can find *rest* in just as a person is. In this place sense I like sometimes to live move and have my being in some place the circumstances relative to which *seem* remote from me because of their extreme difference from what I usually choose. But it is often the case that great concentration and liking for one thing will give me a special capacity for liking something quite different. But in my case the difference is made more poignant by the fact that my liking for it is found to be based on a liking I have for my usual and more familiar abodes, namely my being able to make some sort of home or nest in it; in my being able to find myself in it. This is the case I think with the landscapes I call 'group four'. To this group in addition to the foreign country group . . . belongs also those landscapes that have this remote from me quality . . .

In all of these landscapes I have more or less only been a camera: a camera that had some inkling of what I liked, and which arranged everything in about the point of view and angle I should want when I want to consider the next stage, namely a figure painting. They are and needed to be extremely elaborate studies as when the time came for me when this or that place was to be the place factor in the painting I might not be there or able to get there. I don't like, especially in regard to Cookham, to consider such possibilities but it is a fact that I have been these later years away from Cookham and having photos of these land-scapes is most important to me. As I have explained I selected those places to do from the point of view of being places I liked to imagine people being in, those people being my own particular brand of people that I like.

733.2.422; dated 28 September 1948, in which Spencer describes his imaginative work as 'the marriage of some external me thing with some internal one'.

It was less easy to avoid being precipitated into doing landscapes than might be thought. The thought that I should be dependent for my living by the sale of such paintings as 'Apple Gatherers' (p27) and the like – any of which demanded an eternity – caused a kind of paralysis – I longed to do such things without feeling the financial pressure. The doing landscape and ready sale thereof might relieve that pressure. It did not. Then there were these long spaces of time when circumstances were not such as I seem to need, in order to do the work I like and hope to do. The great and chief bug bear of my 1911 and 1919 to 1923 days was no fire in winter and the landscape doing demand in the summer. Doing landscape or still life etc was possibly as unsuited to me as it might have been to Blake. I don't know if he ever did any. I like very much of course any incidental landscape 'bit' in my figure pictures as for instance in the Zacharias and in others or the land-scape that occurs in Blake's work.

Places to me were uninhabited Heavens, and as such seemed unrealizable and unattainable, and somehow not convincing.

But somehow by wandering through this desert and almost not me landscape vale I find it a means to discover my mental whereabouts. I was longing to get back from Durweston and begin the 'Christ Carrying the Cross' (p35) painting which was now clear and ready to do. And I was standing about in Mr Draper's orchard watching the cricket in the evening after the arduous day of landscape painting was done. The worst of the landscape business was that it so much emphasised the distance between my landscape viewpoint and imaginative urge as to drive them ever further apart. Much as my outdoor everyday life was via landscape painting it seemed to make my imaginative world more and more interior, more and more unable to reach the real life blood that now seemed to be growing its way in my landscape work and doing so to no purpose because it didn't fuse with the landscape work, only inha-bited that region of my work.

I was just able to hold on to the meaning I need to give myself the degree of urge I look for in doing such imagi-native work as I did in 1920–23 up to which time I had done the composition for the Tate Resurrection and for most of the Burghclere memorial. Landscapes have been done by me when and where there was little or no imagi-native experience as in the cases and places I have des-

Farm Pond, Leonard Stanley 1940, Tate Gallery (not in display)

cribed and where and when I subsequently did them. I wish to describe my next 'touch down' to do landscapes and you will see they have little or nothing to do with my imaginative life. I will describe something where my interior imaginative longing led me to some outdoor happening which was let us say the superficial or exterior paraphernalia of my doing some imaginative composition. I am in Cookham and I like a certain orchard and I look through the high bars. The way to the left seems to go nowhere. It seems to be a part of what I am looking for. I go with my cousin to feed a calf in a shed in this orchard and in time, some while afterwards I do the 'Girl feeding calf' (Jas Ward has it) and the path to the left in 'The Nativity' (Slade) arises from the cogitations about that path. I didn't do any drawing of it. I think about it and it seems to become a part of my joy and in the same way identified with things buried in myself. It is in my thought and I am in my own 'Fernlea' home, and becomes so much a part of that inner reality as to seem to become, because now so personal, hardly credible as an external thing, a place to which I can walk. In the midst of the thoughts I walk to it and look again through the high bars, and return and wander again into the thoughts about it. The exercise of performing the marriage of some external me thing with some internal one.

But at Bourne End when I return from Durweston it is still summer and I bathe near Spade Oak and sometime I and MS punt up to 'the Nile' as they called it and bathe off an island. Not a Cookham-like island, but a Robinson Crusoeish one and we walk about on it in the long dried up grass . . .

But all such happenings as these had no place in my work. I wish they did but there is not the time for all my experience to be realized and unfortunately some of that daily experience involves painting what has not been by me mentally digested.

733.2.370 begun January 16th 1948, in which Spencer accounts for the 'links and joins' in his life, when personal circumstances diverted him into producing landscapes. Wishes he could have enjoyed painting them as much as he enjoys writing about them, which he does, he suggests, as a kind of 'confession'. But it is human beings, not objects, which are the source of expression 'of all the religious spiritual meanings'.

My Feelings about 'Anna Karenina'

It's all compiling and weaving, not a conception as far as I can see.
Like Dickens he does not seem to understand his job quite. It may be that a very part of one's vision, is the practical ordering and marshalling of material. But if that is so one must feel it as you read it and I didn't. One must feel as one passes from one scene to another and in the passing something of the sonorous music of the whole theme. In Anna Karenina these changes seem pointless jumps . . . If a concept can all the time be felt in this pedestrian-connoisseur-arranging-his-stuff-sort-of-thing-way well and good but I feel that such a writer simply does not know what a concept is and what in writing it does so that that feel of the concept is absent . . .

Well for T [Dudley Tooth, Spencer's dealer] I am supposed to be a landscape painter. Supposed to be because I do them. Now let us consider a host of other suppositions and mistaken notions that may arise in the onlooker's mind from that. He sees them, their variety of place and kind and here follows a list of possible supposings:
1. He supposes I would select
2. That my going to this and that place would arise from the fact that I had heard of its beauty, or because of some interesting paintable factor.
3. He might in wishing to be a landscape painter himself and to show 'proper taste' like painting in the Constable Country, wish to visit my 'haunts'. He might as I did travel all across Europe doing landscapes in Sarajevo etc. It might give him a pause when he comes to the fact that I painted Landscapes in Halifax. He would overcome that jolt with concluding that possibly the red sandstone was effective and off he would go. Now what would he be doing? He would in fact be going through the geographical part of the domestic circumstances of my life minus the exigences that produced them, namely wars and women. If he *liked* those landscapes of mine he would have to know and understand that roughly speaking troublous wars and ditto women are very much the technique of them.

I am telling the story of this complacent stream of landscapes. Suspension of what I am doing and want to do. Money need. Doggedness.

Are among the various elements that make them . . .

He was depressed and his whole spiritual trend had received a terrific snub and setback. His figure pictures in which he put his whole being such as it was, were a hope and a trust and a seal in his (not merely belief) but his rejoicing in the world's regeneration and redemption. His pictures were (as he hoped) declarations of peace. A feeling of, no, this is *not* the acceptable year of the Lord, get back to your kennel or as you Hilda would say, tunnel. He saw that the time was not propitious for singing 'Hail the bridegroom hail the bride'. Nothing other than complacence could produce another 'Zacharias'. Anyway whether he should or should not have done he felt the all withering and icy blast of the war. He could still *believe* in a world of great joy outside himself, but he was dependent on it also. The bridegroom was gone and a time of fasting had come. He felt suspended. Question was how and in what way to hibernate. Was he wrong so to feel and do, possibly yes I only state the facts. He felt he had got to fit in somehow. Felt shamed that another brother [Gilbert Spencer] was able to fit in and lose none of his spiritual grip. He did landcapes and so thinks Stanley must I . . .

Emulous influences causing and directing the production of my first two landcapes. One, the change from my religious imaginary pictures to landscape caused by war depression and two, selections caused by competitive copycat of brother. Auspicious introduction to landscape painting, what? I am not liking to confess this as it is such impudent presumption that I should ever have supposed I could do what he did . . .

There are as a fact in life and part of the truth of it these links and joins, even the vast 1914–18 war experience was not enough to break me of the emulous business re brother and the disturbance of the war experience had its effects until some year after its end. Being so easily blown away and blowable away from what I prior to it had purposed and felt convinced was my job, and the starting again needed a recovery of that confidence, I again was in listless lost state and during this time felt that if I was a man of genius as others seem to think, I must be so at any moment and occasion. So that while I at least did manage to get to doing the paintings I wanted to do (the big ones) I felt on some occasions when I went for a stay with HL [Henry Lamb] and brother [Gilbert] in Dorset (in 1920 or 21) that as *they* went out landscape painting and as it seemed not the time for this gestating period of needing to think about some notion, I also must do landscape. I felt a challenge, instead of realising I could only do what I could do, I fancied myself able to do what I found I could not

and again got the pip very badly. It took me so long to do *one* that HL seeing me out after dusk, still at it, suggested I took a lantern. It was a sort of reunion of soldiers after the war occasion, HL had asked G and I to stay with him. So far so good but I could not get my mind on what I wanted to do and so there was this miniature suspension of me similar to the Great War suspension I had just emerged from. So utterly not what I was *feeling* did I find what I was *doing* that I felt a need to see that the two things, feeling and doing were kept well and clearly apart. I did not want my own inward pet feelings to experience this outward blizzard and deliberately selected unhappy things to paint namely things in which my own feeling and happiness had not entered or been able to enter . . .

I kept things apart for this reason –
1. I saw that to earn I would have to do them
2. That I had no wish or intention ever to be able to be fully expressive by means of painting an object in front of me. Mercifully for me such occupation was not pertinent to my work and aim. It was just that there came times in my life, disturbing times when periods of suspension forced upon me and when nevertheless I had to 'work' and earn money. My early emulousness rewarded with later finding myself involved in *having* to do landscape or starve and let those dependent on me starve. Some may think I should have done so. I am only stating facts. I *did* do those landscapes because of what I have above explained (envy and war) and later to get money. Whether I loved money more than I loved to give my whole undivided time to those early figure religious pictures and to cogitating about them I leave others to say, armen. No, not armen, only I may have to chuck this in order to have my rest and it may change my present rollicking style of diction. I wish I could have enjoyed doing the landscapes as I enjoy writing about them. It is probably a relief of the mental strain I underwent in doing them. The confessor's relief in confessing, no I don't think so. There may be something of that in it however. It's funny that this landscape side of my life in writing my life seems a balancing help. If along with my soul I go too deep into matters the reader can say 'he'll have to surface sooner or later he has got to do a landscape' and we readers can gauge a lot from those surfacings. Well now we will just pad (padding) a bit Mr T[ooth] if you don't mind otherwise I shall be polishing off my landscape story in another half page. I'll spin this part out a bit by relating the doing of the about six landscapes I did at Durweston in Dorset that time. Only I must have my rest (read 'Anna') and do my shopping. Being Saturday I must get week's rations. Pity. Often these things break the thread. Be ready thread for the picking up. Don't break.

[continues in different handwriting, different pencil]

When faced by an object in being deprived of my happiness and the emotions going with it I am also deprived of any *sense* of proportion which sense I do to a certain extent attain to in my other work. By that I don't mean I get my measurements wrong in a landscape in a practical way, but that the *sense* of relative size etc is not there, the drama of it is not there. Naturally because drama is tucked away along with other feelings. That may or may not be the cause, can't say. What I don't love and feel I can make no interesting comment upon . . .

While at Bourne End the B's [Behrends] who had for years been patrons of mine came to see their friends with whom I stayed. I had always believed that when the B's bought the big religious paintings of mine, 'Swan Upping' (p13) and 'The Cowls' ['Mending Cowls, Cookham' p10] that in their liking for these things they were identified with me and my liking for them.

I, hating and detesting these landcapes was therefore somewhat shocked when to my surprise the B's so much liked them that they bought three of them, the only three that were there. Mollified and gratified at having the much needed money I revelled in the financial relief. But I did think well. So much for the approbation I had had for the other stuff. If say 'The Cowls' is of no more moment than say one of those landscapes then I have greatly overestimated my powers. Being my own best judge saves me from that conclusion . . .

I am sure of securing what I am after namely a thing in which all is fused and is one.

The contemplation in my mind of human beings and all the whole range of what being a human being means to me and through that contemplation realising and longing for the expression of all the religious spiritual meanings that are there to be reached and achieved especially intensifies my wish and desire to express the exact identity of what I love in them. As I pointed out before, the design element in my pictures is the shape of my love. I am wanting and hoping for a time when I can have my jaws reticulated so that I can swallow a human being whole without it having to be mis-shaped in order to fit into my design, fit into my love scheme. A thing to be enjoyed by me spiritually may have here and there to be a visible thing exterior to myself and to be observed by me. The practical fact as I have pointed out before of observing things involves the purely physical fact that some things and aspects of life outside oneself are more easily observ-able than others. In landscape there are all sorts of changes and happenings but the happenings respecting human beings especially troubles: I mean the practical and ordinary psychological ones. 1. The fact that they move. 2. The fact that they are often annoyed at being looked at and observed and at once become suspicious if I begin to draw them. If I have them in my room it is not only what I want I am also very nervous of asking.

733.8.2 two passages on his 'nudes', discussed in relation to other works, the first undated, in which he lists them and describes an improvised arrangement of them placed around his room. The second is dated 26 April 1947, in which he places the nude section in the context of his Church-House scheme, and outlines the 'subjects' of other rooms. A third passage dated September 1955 on Double Nude Portrait, 1936 is on p45.

I wish my shows could include the nudes (oil) that I have done. I think to have them interspersed in a show would convey the range of my work. They are quite different. I wish there were more of them, but I have never had pro[fessional] models, not liking the idea. I believe I could do some good painting if I did. If I got enough done I would have a show. They have such an effect on the other works. I have not done any for years now. I only did them in about 1933/5. The list of names is:
1. 'Sitting in armchair' 30 × 20 P ['Nude, Portrait of Patricia Preece', 1935, Ferens Art Gallery, Hull]
2. 'Lying Down' 20 × 30 P ['Nude, Portrait of Patricia Preece', 1935, Ivor Braka Limited, London p22]
3. 'Semi-nude' 24 × 36 P ['Patricia Preece', 1936, private collection]
4. 'Double nude' 24 × 36 P and S ['Self-Portrait with Patricia Preece', 1936, Fitzwilliam Museum, Cambridge p44]
5. 'Double nude' approx 40 × 40 P and S ['Double Nude Portrait: The Artist and his Second Wife', 1937, Tate Gallery p45]
6. 'Sitting on Sofa' 30 × 20 H ['Seated Nude, Hilda', 1936–42, private collection, see drawing p42]
7. 'Lying on Back' 24 × 36 P ['Patricia Preece', private collection]
No 6 I did from a drawing I did in 1929 (about). In the drawing there is an African necklace. No 7 I drew in pencil from P and just began to paint and then gave it up. That was about 1936 or 37. In 1942 I finished it from the pencil drawing that I could still see on the canvas. I painted it entirely from the drawing except about four square inches. I want to be able to paint a nude from life and to do it as I do a portrait. I mean not so quickly but taking my time. The No 1 'Sitting in the armchair' is the best in that respect. The head does not properly belong to the body: I was trying to squeeze it into a 30 × 20. This

21

Nude, Portrait of Patricia Preece 1935 (p44)

was painted at Lindworth in about 1935 or thereabouts. All the others were painted there except that the last two were done in the studio and without any model, as I say one from a drawing and the other being drawn on canvas. I would like to get back from Tooth's the large double-nude they apparently didn't show. Also the 1. Old Couple, 2. The Thin ditto, 3. The Consciousness Couple, 4. The Seeing Couple, 5. Desire and 6. Contemplation. I think they or someone they have lent it to have the semi-nude, unless it was sold. I don't think it was.

The nudes are completely different from the figure pictures, as is, of course all the works I do from some object, as for instance portraits and still lifes. I have the No 7 'Lying on Back' here and I have been putting it along with the Resurrection paintings. I put round the room just what I had and I feel the need of these paintings from life: I wish I could paint all I do from life, especially the figure pictures, or rather mix the breed. When I looked at this 'show' I had, I could feel something of this mixture. The show I will again arrange as follows.

Under window 1. three 30×20 canvases making the Resurrection scene where the grave-tenders see children who have just resurrected rejoicing. Then narrow chest of drawers between this and next window and on it leaning against wall a large coloured repro of 2. 'The Bridal Path' landscape. As the 'dumb waiter' (brought from Catesbury 13 shillings in about 1928 and now storing my and Hilda's writing from 1920 to 1933) is under the second window and is in line with the aforesaid chest of drawers I have leant the next painting 3. 'The window and street Resurrection' against it. The central and left side 30×20 panel only are done at present. The central panel 30×35 is canvas pinned to a drawing board and awaiting stretcher. Against the projecting bit of board where the right 30×20 panel will go when painted I have leant the 30×20 panel I call 4. 'Toasting'. It is supposed to be an imagined notion I have of H[ilda] and I nude by the fire and making toast: I painted it in early part of 1938. Then pinned against wall same side to right of right window 5. a nude pencil drawing of myself. The drawing is over seven feet high. Now on wall at right angles to this wall and in same corner another eight feet tall nude pencil drawing of myself. This one is front view and the other was side view or three quarters. Next to this comes 6. 'The Hill of Zion', which

22

takes up most of the side of that wall except for the aforesaid narrow life drawing. Now turn right again and there is the door. To the right of the door (looking from inside the room as we all the time are) comes my table at which I work and over it hanging on the wall is 7. nude 'Lying on Back'. To the right of this and over my bed is 8. 'The Resurrection' where children are combing their mother's hair and tidying them after the resurrection. On the next and last of the four walls there is nothing. It is where the fireplace is. There is also a small painting began of D[aphne], and also a small painting I did from a drawing of a shipbuilding furnace man's head.

26 April 1947
It was when I was writing what I call Church-House, at the time when I hoped to work out a scheme when the Church and church pictures gradated into a house or houses and house and domestic life pictures, and into nature, (other than human nature), landscape, animals, vegetation etc. The Church was to be part of the Cookham Village and part of Cookham and the house parts any interior and happenings therein I liked, and the nature and animals etc parts to be places round about Cookham and also places elsewhere. I wanted in the nude section to show the analogy between the Church and the prescribed nature of worship, and human love. There would be a room of nudes from life and on the way and here and there in the room or in the approaches to it would be paintings of all the things that form the parts of a person such as clothes, underclothes, boots etc. These would be done rather in the form of still life. These stockings etc would be painted as far as I was able in the same spirit and intention as I would also do 'still lifes' of the implements, vesture etc of the New Testament.

The thought of these tentacles reaching out from the traditional Church part of the building to the various aspects of life would to me be very interesting. There would be a room of cattle in the fields and a room of heads.

The room of nudes would show how much they balance a need and the whole cosmical conception. There might be a garden room, and object room and a landscape room.

733.2.375 a draft letter to Hilda, dated 20–21 January 1946 in which Spencer points out that each picture might be painted differently, and yet 'each way' be 'right' for the meaning.

I myself cannot separate the feeling I had about the 'subject' of 'The Betrayal' from the composing and painting the picture I did of it. I cannot find any separation between the thoughts I had about the subject of my Zacharias picture, the lines they [Zacharias and Elizabeth] 'walked in all the commandments and ordinances of the Lord blameless' are with me like a presence all the time I am doing it. I could not look at one part of that picture without seeing that the way it was painted was inseparable from that subject and was directed by it. The way I painted 'The Cowls' picture is in me inseparable from what gave me the wish to paint it, sentiment and association. The same association and subject matter actuates me in painting 'The Centurion's Servant'. Any excellence in the quality of painting in any of these things arises direct from that emotion. I cannot separate the subject of Christ carrying the cross from me painting it. If I look at these paintings I find considerable variety in the way they are painted. Look at the differences for instance in 'The Centurion's Servant'; the 'Zacharias' and the 'Christ Carrying the Cross'. The difference does not arise from being in doubt and therefore trying different techniques (so I think) but in each case I am completely assured and happy and yet each is quite different. Each 'way' is right to the picture and the painting and meaning.

STANLEY SPENCER

1891–1959

1891
Born 30 June at Cookham-on-Thames, Berkshire, the eighth surviving child of Anna and William Spencer, organist and piano teacher.

1896–1906
Educated at home.

1907
Studied art at Maidenhead Technical Institute.

1908–12
Studied art at the Slade School, London under Henry Tonks. Continued to live and paint at home, commuting to London for his classes. Awarded a scholarship, 1910; the Melville Nettleship Prize and the Composition Prize, 1912.

1913–14
Living at 'Fernlea', produces his first important works.

1915–18
Enlisted in the Royal Army Medical Corps. Posted to Macedonia in August 1916 and served with Field Ambulances until August 1917, where he volunteered and joined the 7th Battalion, the Royal Berkshires. Commissioned as an official War Artist to paint one picture on his return to England in December 1918.

1919
Lived and worked in Cookham. Member of the New English Art Club until 1927.

1920–21
Lived with Sir Henry and Lady Slesser at Bourne End, near Cookham.

1921–22
Lived with the Muirhead Bones at Steep, near Petersfield, Hampshire.

1922
Visited Yugoslavia with the Carline family during the summer. Moved to Hampstead in December.

1923–24
Enrolled at the Slade School for the spring term 1923. Then stayed with Henry Lamb at Poole, Dorset, where Mr and Mrs J L Behrend saw his designs for the mural decoration of a chapel commemorating his war experience. They commission a chapel to be built at Burghclere.

1925
Married Anna Hilda Carline, a painter, at Wangford, near Southwold on February 3. A daughter, Shirin, born.

1926–27
Completed 'The Resurrection, Cookham' in 1926 and exhibited it in his first one-man show at the Goupil Gallery, London, in 1927. It was purchased by Lord Duveen for presentation to the Tate Gallery. Moved to Burghclere to start decorating the Sandham Memorial Chapel.

1930
A second daughter, Unity, born.

1932
Completed the Sandham Memorial Chapel and moved to 'Lindworth', Cookham. Elected Associate of the Royal Academy and exhibits five paintings and five drawings at the Venice Biennale. In October Dudley Tooth becomes his sole agent.

1933
Invited to Switzerland, by Edward Beddington-Behrens, to paint landscapes.

1935
Resigned from the Royal Academy when the hanging committee rejected two of his entries for the Summer Exhibition.

1936
Visited Switzerland again with Beddington-Behrens.

1937
Divorced by Hilda Carline. Married Patricia Preece, also a painter, at Maidenhead Registry Office.

1939–40
Stayed intermittently at the White Hart Inn, Leonard Stanley, Gloucestershire, with George and Daphne Charlton, both of whom were painters.

1940
Commissioned by the War Artists Advisory Committee to paint pictures of shipyards. Made the first of a series of visits to the Lithgow yard, Port Glasgow.

1942–44
Returned to Cookham. Continued to visit Port Glasgow and to work on 'Shipbuilding on the Clyde'. Began 'The Resurrection: Port Glasgow' series on which he worked until 1950.

1947
Retrospective exhibition, Temple Newsam House, Leeds.

1950
Created CBE. Rejoined the Royal Academy and was elected an Academician. Hilda Spencer died in November.

1954
Visited China as a member of a cultural delegation.

1955
Retrospective exhibition at Tate Gallery.

1958
Made Associate of the Royal College of Art.

1959
Knighted. Died 14 December at the Canadian War Memorial Hospital, Cliveden, Berkshire.

CATALOGUE

Dimensions: height followed by width in millimetres.
Numbers prefixed T, N, L, are those of the Tate Gallery catalogue.
733 numbers refer to Tate Gallery Archive.
Page numbers refer to illustrations of the works.

Jacob and Esau   1910–11
Pen, pencil and wash on paper
343 × 241
Bequeathed by Lady Ruth Gollancz 1973
T01769

A Slade Sketch Club set subject, illustrating the story in Genesis 25:29–34, in which Esau sells his birthright as first-born son in exchange for some 'bread and a pottage of lentils'. Spencer makes the comparison between Esau, 'a hairy man', and Jacob, the smooth-skinned and more sophisticated of the two brothers. In May 1942 he wrote: 'I seem, without being conscious of it at the time (or I should say I have no memory of being conscious at the time) . . . of being aware of the psychological situation of the story and yet these two figures seem very good from that psychological point of view. I remember considering the field at the back which was a field down Cliveden and the general wish for that atmosphere to unite with the bible atmosphere but I have nothing but the dimmest memory of the fraud Jacob engaged in, and yet the figures   25 illustrate this aspect well' [733.3.40].

The linear precision of the drawing would have met the exacting demands of a Slade School exercise. Spencer invests it with a Pre-Raphaelite charm and characterisation, familiar to him from reproductions kept around the family home, 'Fernlea'.

gentle melancholy of a visionary moment is seen in both these early works, as in 'Zacharias and Elizabeth', 1914 (p14), in all of which landscape signifies a spiritual context.

Study for *Joachim among the Shepherds*   1912
Pen, pencil and wash on paper
406 × 371
Presented by the Trustees of the Chantrey Bequest 1955
T00048

Man Goeth to his Long Home   1911
Pen, pencil and wash on paper
432 × 318
Purchased 1945
N05608

Another Slade Sketch Club subject, illustrating a passage from the Book of Ecclesiastes, 12:5, 'Also when they shall be afraid of that which is high, and fears shall be in the way, and the almond tree shall flourish, and the grasshopper shall be a burden, and desire shall fail; because man goeth to his long home, and the mourners go about the streets'.

Gilbert Spencer recalled that the landscape background was a view looking south from the corner of Carter's Shed, by Lambert's Stables, Cookham, the same as is used for 'Joachim among the Shepherds', 1912 (below). The

A detailed study for the painting 'Joachim among the Shepherds' (private collection), painted in 1912, shortly after the artist had left the Slade. The treatment of the narrative shows Spencer's absorption in the painting of the early Italian artists whom Ruskin championed. Ruskin's vivid evocations of their work were read aloud in 'Fernlea' by his father. Spencer was given a copy of Ruskin's book on the Arena Chapel, *Giotto and his Works in Padua*, which he said had influenced his composition. In one edition of Ruskin's *Works* (Cook and Wedderburn, XXIV, p50) the following quotation appears alongside a woodcut after Giotto's composition 'Joachim retires to the Sheepfold': 'Then Joachim, in the following night, resolved to separate himself from companionship; to go to the desert places among the mountains, with his flocks; and to inhabit those mountains, in order not to hear such insults. And immediately Joachim rose from his bed, and called about him all his servants and shepherds, and caused to be gathered together all his flocks . . . and went with them and with the shepherds into the hills'.

Later Spencer wrote: 'The pathway in this picture is taken from a pathway in Cookham that leads from the west end of Cookham Village to the Strand Castle. This depicts the occasion when Joachim goes to live with the Shepherds' (733.3.16). And again: 'I liked to take my thoughts for a walk and marry them to some place in Cookham. The "bread and cheese" hedge up the Strand ash-path was the successful suitor. There was another hedge going away at right angles from the path and this was where the shepherds seemed to be. We had to walk single-file along this path and the shadows romped about in the hedge alongside of us. And I liked the hemmed-in restricted area feeling in that open land . . . That endless path! Could nothing be done to "jolly" it up? And then Joachim and the shepherds gave it their blessing, and saved me from getting bored'. (Carline, p28)

In the final painting (for which an oil sketch also exists) the figure of Joachim is brought into the foreground, and the trellis and landscape background replaced by an arch of foliage. This drawing, signed and dated, was shown at the winter exhibition of the New English Art Club, as 'Joachim among the Sheepcotes'. The subject exerted enough fascination for Spencer to produce a woodcut and watercolour of the same. In a notebook of 1937, the artist wrote that it was painted in the front bedroom of 'Fernlea' and under the heading: 'Notes on the subject matter of my pictures', provides his own personal caption for the work: 'The Strand. Seeing familar objects such as bread and cheese, leaves of the hedge under my own auspices and in a world of my own creating'.

Study for *The Apple Gatherers*   c1912
Pen, pencil and wash on paper
276 × 321
Bequeathed by Sir Edward Marsh through the
Contemporary Art Society 1954
N06233

This is probably the drawing Spencer made for the Slade Sketch Club, for which he won £25. Squared for transfer, it is similar in design to the painting, but the artist made several changes. In the finished picture, the space between the figures is greatly reduced, and the whole composition pressed forward to fill the canvas, an indication of his increasingly bold approach. In addition, the arms and interlocking hands of the central man and women are made a focal point, instead of dropping into shadow, as here. Similarly, the lighting in the painting emphasises the muscular arm of the woman in the foreground, her male counterpart's position having been changed to mirror her own.

Apple Gatherers   1912–13
Oil on canvas
714 × 924
Presented by Sir Edward Marsh 1946
N05663

A Slade Sketch Club set subject, for which Spencer's prize-winning drawing survives (left). He worked on the painting for over a year, and it remained, in his view, one of his most significant works. The originality of the conception is matched by the ambitious formal design which may have been influenced by his friend Henry Lamb's interest in Gauguin and the Pont Aven School.

The fact that many Slade subjects were biblical might

have suggested the theme of Adam and Eve, though Spencer resisted too literal an interpretation of his picture. 'There is no symbolic meaning whatsoever intended in 'Apple Gatherers', and I cannot account for the fact that I have divided the sexes in the picture' (733.3.1). If there was no specific symbolic meaning, there was however a meditation on a constant preoccupation: 'It is significant to me that in my early religious pictures done at a time when I was innocent I wanted to include in the concept the idea of men and women, something that does go past and beyond the usual conceptions to whatever the relationship is' (733.3.21).

It was 'a place on Odney Common where looking towards a grassy bank towards Mill Lane I had the feeling for that picture'. There was no orchard there but 'it was the place I thought about because it seemed to bring the thought of this picture in my mind. It helped me to the frame of mind to produce this idea' (733.3.16). Spencer's feeling for place was thus an integral part of his imaginative figure paintings. Writing in 1936, he recalled: 'When at the end of each day it had begun to get too dark to paint in the kitchen of 'Wisteria' where . . . I was painting 'Apple Gatherers', I used, sometimes to stand on a little landing . . . and look from the cottage window to the still bare branches of some spindle-like trees which were hidden in the confusion of overgrown yew hedge and other shrub-stuff, and there watch and listen to a blackbird which could be seen in the dusk, making a little darkness . . . among those few criss-crossing twigs and thin branches; the notes sounded more local and imminent as darkness came on' (Carline p34).

Spencer used his own muscular arms and hands for both the male and female figures in the foreground, and his own mouth in the faces of the young men on the right. The interlocked arms and hands of the two central figures are made a focus of the erotic charge of the imagery. Here the artist was able to combine two of his abiding concerns: male/female coupling and the sanctity of place, in a fusion of the sacred and the sexual.

In a note of c1939–40, Spencer linked the love feeling of this picture to other early works: 'It is also to me significant of this desire in me to rescue the love interest from its usual context in people's mind when I consider the motive of 'Apple Gatherers' which feels and conveys something of the wonder and mystery of men and women and of the possibility of its meaning, and the quite natural way I am moved by the husband and wife subject of Zacharias. The passionate couple behind the railing in 'The Nativity' and the sense of homeliness in the 'The Centurion's Servant' and love of servants' (733.3.20).

Self-Portrait 1912
Red chalk on paper
395 × 219
Williamson Art Gallery and Museum, Birkenhead

One of several drawings relating to the oil 'Self-Portrait' of 1913. The use of red chalk for a detailed life study reveals Spencer's traditional Slade training. Tonks, the much feared Slade tutor, wrote to the family after Spencer left the School: 'In some ways he has shown signs of having the most original mind of anyone we have had at the Slade'. Here the artist depicts an interior gaze, quite different from the confident projection of the oil painting.

Self-Portrait 1913
Oil on canvas
629 × 508
Bequeathed by Sir Edward Marsh through the
Contemporary Art Society 1953
N06188 (p6)

Spencer's first painted self-portrait, made when the artist was aged 22, took nearly a year to complete. At one and a half times life-size, it is a clear declaration of intent. The tilted angle of the mirror he looks into throws his head high and erect. The picture is referred to by the artist in a letter to Henry Lamb 7 May 1914: 'I must go now and go on with my portrait that is getting on at last'. When Edward Marsh, who bought the picture, asked him why it was so big, Spencer replied: 'Next time I start a portrait I shall begin it the size of a threepenny bit' (Carline, p39). Marsh was nonetheless convinced of Spencer's talents: 'How I admire Stan's Self-Portrait now finished! His portrait is to me nothing short of a masterpiece. It glows with warm, but reserved feeling and has the dignity of an old master in it. And he has done the whole of it with penny brushes! (Sydney Spencer, diary, 7 July 1914, quoted in Pople, p50n).

Zacharias and Elizabeth 1914
Oil on canvas
1700 × 1703
Private Collection (p14)

The narrative was described by Spencer in 1959: 'Zacharias appears in the foreground at an altar. Sweeping down on him is an imagined angel. Further back among the grass and just by an old yew hedge Zacharias appears again with Elizabeth. Elizabeth has her arm crooked, and rests it on a tray-like frond of the yew. Her hand disappears into the tree. Behind the wall and to the left is a kneeling figure and above the wall in the top of the picture just by the sky is another head and shoulders of a figure. She is Elizabeth again, on her own, just as Zacharias is alone (with the angel), as he is making his sacrifice. It just wanted someone in that juncture of the wall and the greenhouse'.

Spencer began the picture in December 1913, writing to his friend Henry Lamb: 'I have a big square canvas . . . I am going to have it out on this canvas if it's the last act, as Brer Rabbit would say' (Carline, pp36–37). In March he invited Lamb to come to see 'my big Zacharias picture just begun'.

The location chosen by Spencer was the garden of Wisteria Cottage, where he had a studio. The back of the cottage overlooked the gardens of St George's Lodge, which ran down to the Thames. He painted the view from memory, altering the scene as necessary: 'The high wall seen from the back window of 'Wisteria', although Cookham and a particular part of it that I liked, was not quite personal enough for me' (733.3.375). He transformed the wall making it a smooth curved expanse, one of the most memorable structures in his entire work. It provoked uncomprehending criticism. P G Konody, the art critic of the *Observer*, expressed both grudging admiration and sarcasm in his assessment of the picture when it was exhibited at the New English Art Club in 1920: 'It is not a picture to be dismissed with an impatient shrug', he wrote, 'for it has that sense of awe that makes unquestionably a very powerful and direct sense of appeal, quite apart from the charming landscape background painted with a Pre-Raphaelite's love of elaborate detail. But the picture gains nothing from the grotesque treatment of the figures . . . Zacharias himself being disguised as a chef . . . If the buildings and ruins of the Giottesques often lacked architectural stability, the primitive painters nevertheless did their best to make their walls look like walls. In Mr Spencer's picture the . . . screen-like erection behind the central group looks more like a portion of an enamel bath than like a wall' (*Observer*, 4 January 1920).

Spencer later wrote that Zacharias was 'the only weak thing in the picture and is the most important thing so that picture is a very good shell and nothing in it or worse still contains a vamped up piece of cooking. When I was doing it everything came clearly and fairly simply except that figure and finally I merely inserted a figure instead of leaving an empty space' (733.3.22). It is clear, however, that the picture held special significance for him. Looking back he wrote: 'Nothing other than complacence could produce another Zacharias' (733.2.370).

In conversation with John Rothenstein, Spencer confirmed his high regard for this picture and his early 'Self-Portrait' (p6) as belonging to a period of particular inspiration: 'Those pictures have something that I have lost. When I left the Slade and went back to Cookham I entered a kind of earthly paradise. Everything seemed fresh and to belong to the morning. My ideas were beginning to unfold in fine order when along comes the war and smashes everything. When I came home the divine sequence had gone. I just opened a shutter in my side and out rushed my pictures anyhow. Nothing was ever the same again' (Rothenstein, 1984, pp95–96).

The Centurion's Servant 1914
Oil on canvas
1143 × 1143
Presented by the Trustees of the Chantrey Bequest 1960
T00359

Painted in the schoolroom at the back of 'Fernlea' and 'The Nest' and in 'The Ship Cottage'. The bible story is from Luke 7:1–10, and is traditionally seen as an example of absolute faith. In connection with this painting, Spencer wrote that he painted his pictures 'trustingly'.

The artist had planned a companion picture depicting the meeting between Christ and the Centurion's messenger. Spencer's idea was to show the man in a walking position, which would echo the position of the recovering servant. 'This seemed beyond me; but I began to find my mind in very outdoor places in trying to imagine what this scene would be like. I vaguely remember willows and sunlight in certain parts of Cookham. In that baffled state my mind wandered off to some shade and in doing so I wondered what the scene would be actually at the house where the servant was, seven miles away. Here I seemed to get a better foot hold. I don't think it struck me then as it does now that the room that I selected as being the bedroom in which this servant was to suddenly revive was our own servant's bedroom; I mean that they were both servants and both in bedrooms. Perhaps the Centurion servant being a male made a difference' (733.3.21).

The companion panel was never executed. But despite the difficulties in realising his full intentions, Spencer later wrote that he had 'a fine and clear concept', for 'The Centurion's Servant', which he affectionately referred to

as his 'Bed Picture'. In a notebook of c1940, the artist wrote: 'I am still mentally in that house', and again 'I painted the picture in 1914 and I am still thinking about it. But although I am satisfied with it what I had in mind and what may have started me in the direction of painting it never came off' (733.9.133).

With the biblical narrative Spencer fuses 'a few circumstances of my own life and surroundings at the time when I did the picture which to me increased the meaning I was seeking.' He recalls the local custom whereby villagers used to gather to pray round the bedside of those who were ill; and his own praying positions in church ('I used to gaze around the church while praying and feel the atmosphere I was praying in'). He describes, in one passage, how he used to hear voices coming from the servant's room at 'Fernlea', thinking the maid was talking to some angel (when in fact he later learnt she was speaking through the wall to the servant next door). 'When the servant came down in the afternoon . . . I would not have been surprised to see her face shine as Moses did when he came from Mount Saine' (733.10.63).

'The Centurion's Servant' is the first instance of the artist visualising himself into the picture (the boy in the middle resembles the young Spencer). It contains some of the artist's most abiding preoccupations: a safe, enclosed space in which the known and familiar is imagined so as to generate a sense of the unknown and unfamiliar. It also (in his words) combines the domestic 'sense of homeliness' and 'love of servants' with his church feelings of 'peace and contentment'.

Mending Cowls, Cookham 1914
Oil on canvas
1092 × 1092
Presented by the Trustees of the Chantrey Bequest 1962
T00530 (p10)

'These Malt houses could be seen from the back window of my old home. In a certain sense I appear to have attained . . . the as I think important meaning they had for me through my not ever being of an enquiring mind. It is so to speak through *not* being a bright or intelligent child that the malt houses just grew into my mind without my having the least idea what they were or what their purpose was. I think the *not* asking what their purpose was would be due to the fact that what was there, over the wall on the right satisfied me. There has to be a logic and reason before any creative work can be done' (733.6.36).

'This child appreciation however *was* dependent on those cowls having a useful and reasonable purpose because when later in life I understood what they were for it heightened my early feeling for them' (733.2.321).

Spencer wrote to his friend Jas Wood about the picture in May 1916, when Wood was thinking of purchasing it. 'I can quite understand you having some misgivings when you saw it as it has a sort of "suppressed emotions" tendency. But I did that thing not because of the "composition" it made; some people say it had a "fine sense of composition", such people know nothing of the feelings which caused me to paint it. There are certain children in Cookham, certain corners of roads and these cowls. All give me one feeling only. I am always wanting to express that' (Tate Archive Microfiche 19).

Elsewhere he described his feelings about the cowls: 'They seemed to be always looking at something or somewhere. When they veered round towards us, they seemed to be looking at something above our own nursery window, and when they turned away to be looking down. The earth by the base of these very big malthouse buildings was never visited by us, so that they were a presence in the midst of the maze of Cookham. From wherever seen, they were somehow benign. With their white wooden heads, they served as reminders of a religious presence' (Carline, p44).

During the second world war, Port Glasgow reminded Spencer of his early affection for Cookham, 'then I could feel my spiritual way just as I did in Cookham. The same love that saw the malt house cowls from our 'Fernlea' window sees now the curved tops of Hamiltons' (733.2.257).

which was to be the abode for all I wished to put in it' (733.2.44).

What he then 'put in it' was the annual swan upping ceremony, held in August, when officials of the Companies of Vintners and Dyers came to collect the swans for marking. To this activity he adds villagers turning over the punts and the Bailey girls carrying cushions.

The picture was begun on 24 March 1915 in the attic of 'The Ship Cottage' Cookham. Spencer had completed only the top two-thirds when he enlisted in the Royal Army Medical Corps. The intervening period 'seriously interfered with the painting of it'. He longed to get back to finish his picture but, 'As an infantry man what would have been the use of this insignificant fragment of gunfodder that I was if I had said to the sergeants "I have a picture at home and I just want to finish it before going into this attack" . . . It can be imagined what I felt when I did at last in fact walk into my bedroom at home and see this picture leaning with its face to the wall on the far side of the big bed' (733.2.44).

Spencer wrote that it was 'a very difficult matter getting back to this painting' and regretted that its completion was not done 'with the care and intensity with which I had begun it . . . The nearest water could have been more water than I made it. I could not seem to get on with drawing and dimly remember attempting to draw the two young daughters of the then proprietors of the Crown Hotel' (733.2.128). But at least, Spencer was satisfied, 'the vision is there'.

Swan Upping at Cookham 1914–19
Oil on canvas
1480 × 1162
Presented by the Friends of the Tate Gallery 1962
T00525 (p13)

Like 'The Centurion's Servant', this picture fuses Spencer's imaginative response to a place, with several personal associations. He recalled that 'the thought in my mind of going on the river was somewhat different from the actual experience. If I was for instance in a pew in the Church just behind this scene in the picture and it was while the 11 o'clock Sunday morning service was proceeding, my mind would be thinking of many things and the effect of being in Church would be affecting my thoughts so that all my thoughts and feelings were a little different from what they were when outside'. To him, the village was part of the Church as much as the Church was part of the village. The river became 'the special part of my mind

Travoys Arriving with Wounded Soldiers at a Dressing Station at Smol, Macedonia, September 1916 1919
Oil on canvas
1830 × 2185
The Trustees of the Imperial War Museum

In a letter to Hilda in the summer of 1923, Spencer recalled the moment which inspired this great picture of his experience of war: 'I was standing a little way from the old Greek church, which was used as a dressing station and operating theatre, and coming there were rows of travoys and limbers crammed full of wounded men. One would have thought that the scene was a sordid one, a terrible scene . . . but I felt there was a grandeur . . . all those wounded men were calm and at peace with everything, so that pain seemed a small thing with them. I felt there was a spiritual ascendancy over everything . . . Like Christ on the Cross [the wounded] belonged to a different world than those tending them . . . I have tried to express the fact that these men on stretchers and the orderlies attending them are inserting peace in the face of war by means of the way I display them in the composition, so that in spite of what is going on and although they are conforming to the conditions they are in . . . nevertheless all seemed to be taking part in some communion of peace. In the top of the picture mules look in at the enlarged window . . . inside of which an operation is in progress. The mules and travoys are coming from the direction of the hill away to the right and lining up outside this old disused church . . . That sort of holly scrub in the foreground was very profuse in its growth; there were great tracts of country covered with it and, as I have heard, it was evidently an ancient Greek weed. The wounded have their faces covered in little squares of mosquito netting for the moment' (733.3.1).

Spencer painted it for the Ministry of Information, having been commissioned as an Official War Artist in 1918, on the recommendation of his friend and patron Muirhead Bone. Only when he was invalided out of Macedonia, awaiting demobilisation, was he able to take up the commission. Spencer submitted to the Advisory Committee a number of pen and wash studies, including several travoy scenes. These had to be made from memory, for his kit-bag with sketches made at the front had been left behind and lost in Macedonia ('I suppose some Macedonian peasant now has my drawings', he lamented). The artist said that his picture 'is intended to convey a sense of peace in the middle of confusion. The figures on the stretchers treated with the same veneration and awe as so many crucified Jesus Christs, and not as conveying suffering but as conveying a happy atmosphere of peace. Also like Christs on the Cross they belong to another world from those attending them' (733.3.1). On 6 February 1919 he reported that 'the picture is begun and goes apace' and by June it was finished. It was begun in his bedroom at 'Fernlea', and continued in the empty Lambert's Stables, at Moor Hall, where he had more space to work on this, his largest canvas to date. His fee was the substantial sum of £200.

Spencer sent this description of the picture to Edward Marsh: 'Along the bottom of the picture and in the immediate foreground are great thistles. The leaves are large and have great spikes. They have milky lines all over them like variegated holly leaves have. The flowers are mauve and look like great maces. The four wounded I think of as separate groups of nebulae. Each group has the same density but might be four saints enthroned, the stretcher handles being so to speak ornaments' (Pople, p188).

In July 1942, Spencer wrote, 'the Travoys taking so long to paint and to compose represents in me a considerable amount of emotional change and variety of feeling. I was very pleased with several aspects of it in the sense of providing some crucial need I felt. For instance in the men under the blankets and the mules. I like the indoors peacefulness of men under blankets with the small pillows and the nets over their faces backed not by the bedstead back but the hindquarters and clipped and moving tails of mules and all the harness and trappings of the outdoor world in the midst of which this peaceful world was taking place. But there is a certain atmosphere in the picture in which my feeling seems to have found expression in various parts of the painting. I say this because every part I look at brings me right and exactly to the me of that moment and a remembrance of how tense that moment was. While I liked it I did not feel the crucial integrated-with-the-thing feeling when I continued and finished the Swan Upping painting' (733.2.128).

Study for *The Bridge* and other works   1912–20
Pencil and wash on paper
356 × 508
Presented anonymously 1947
N05775

The Bridge   1920
Oil on canvas
1213 × 1226
Presented by the National Art Collections Fund 1942
N05393

Between this and the painting Spencer made several changes, though the final result did not please him. The swimmers under the bridge do not appear in the painting, nor do the half-group of figures seen from the back, in the foreground. He maintained the uniformity of the other figures by clothing them in almost identical three-piece suits, thereby emphasising the curious expressions on their faces.

To the right of the main drawing (illustrated above) are three small studies (not shown): one is also for 'The Bridge', another is perhaps for 'Joachim among the Shepherds' (p26), the third unidentified. On the reverse are two studies of women hanging out washing.

In a note of 1937 headed *People on Cookham Bridge*, the artist wrote a retrospective commentary on this picture: 'Still quite at a loss and cannot get my bearings at all. Staying at Slessers because I am constantly interrupted at home and have no room to myself. Quite a good idea of people leaning over either side of bridge and crossing to look from one side to the other, but somehow I felt suspended and could get no grip. Further disturbed by doing it in the Tec' School Maidenhead and put off by having [included] some Jasmin which I saw along King Street. Failed to make it Cookham Bridge and so failed altogether and discarded picture. Still have picture' (733.3.1).

Spencer in fact had to be dissuaded from destroying the picture. It was not shown until the Leicester Galleries exhibition in 1942, when it was dated 1919, and bought by the National Art Collections Fund. Gilbert Spencer pointed out that the quatrefoil stone balustrades were a transcription of the design of Cookham's cast-iron bridge (seen in 'Swan Upping at Cookham'). The dog is 'Tinker', an Airedale terrier belonging to Guy Lacey, a local man who taught the Spencer brothers to swim. Spencer was obliged to use the Maidenhead Technical School as a makeshift studio for large pictures, but shortly after discarding this work, he took up the offer of accommodation at the Slessers, where he was able to work unimpeded and uninterrupted.

The Last Supper   1920
Oil on canvas
914 × 1219
Stanley Spencer Gallery, Cookham, Berkshire

Spencer had made a sketch of this subject in 1915, but only developed it in a pencil and wash study of 1919. Before the war, the artist had discussed the idea of a series of the life of Christ, with his friend Jacques Raverat. It was a project he looked forward to realising: 'When I come home I am going to learn fresco painting and then if Jacques Raverat's project holds good, we are going to build a church, and the walls will have on them all about Christ. If I do not do this on earth, I will do it in Heaven' (Pople, p194). Spencer's opportunity to bring the idea (if not the building scheme) to fruition came when he was invited in 1919 by Margaret and Henry Slesser to work in a room of their house, 'Cornerways', across the river in Bourne End.

On 22 July 1920 Spencer wrote to Henry Lamb that he had finished the picture, but regretted that it 'has not got the nice feeling that the drawing has somehow' (Tate Archive Microfiche 11). The supper takes place inside the malt houses behind 'Fernlea'. The interior of the malt houses may have held a special fascination for the artist since he was forbidden to enter them as a child. He uses the red wall of the grain store as a sort of altar in front of which the figure of Christ presides. St John leans against Christ, whilst Judas, on his left, seems to recoil in embarrassment. Spencer studied the works of the early Italian painters in reproduction in his Gowans and Grays art books, and their influence can be seen in this Giottesque treatment. It is one of his most taut, formal compositions, its symmetrical arrangement emphasised by the two rows of feet up the middle of the picture. (John's Gospel account of the Last Supper begins with Christ washing the disciples' feet, and may have suggested their unusual prominence). Spencer wrote of the picture in

1937: 'I liked the red wall among the sandy coloured ones. Could not get the feeling of the place which at the beginning was indivisible from a concept I had of Christ. It is still there in my mind. But it never came into the picture' (733.3.1). The atmosphere of monastic enclosure nonetheless creates a heightened tension for the drama to unfold.

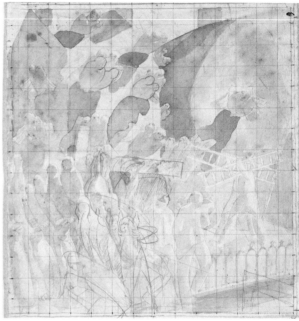

Study for *Christ Carrying the Cross*   1920
Pencil and watercolour on paper
441 × 356
Presented by Mrs Nancy Carline in memory of her husband Richard Carline 1982
T03336

A final study for 'Christ Carrying the Cross', 1920 (right), squared for transfer, in which Spencer's ideas have changed considerably from an earlier, more frontal composition. Christ and the soldiers are moved into the middle ground to give way to the crowd of onlookers, who come and go in every direction. This tonal study stresses the strong shadows cast by the onlookers, and the bold abstract quality of the design. On the left, the artist uses the same fanning arrangement of figures which he had used in 'The Bridge' (p33), painted the same year. Here he attempts to integrate the dynamic arcing lines (which are such a feature of 'The Bridge') with strong verticals and diagonals, to create a dramatically and formally complex composition. The figure of Mary, running with her head down and hands behind her back, was used again by Spencer the following year in 'Christ's Entry into Jerusalem', 1921 (Leeds City Art Galleries).

Christ Carrying the Cross   1920
Oil on canvas
1530 × 1429
Presented by the Contemporary Art Society 1925
N04117

Another of the Passion scenes painted when the artist was staying at Bourne End, as guest of the Slessers. 'Out of

these works the only one I felt at all sure of was 'Christ Carrying the Cross' and to a certain extent with 'The Last Supper''. The cowls of the malt houses (inside which 'The Last Supper' is set) can be glimpsed in the upper left.

His intention for the picture was 'to take the inmost of one's wishes, the most varied religious feeling in one's thought, and to make it an ordinary fact of the street like the edge of the roof'. The event takes place in Cookham High Street, Spencer choosing a viewpoint opposite 'Fernlea' and 'The Nest' (his grandmother's house) to observe the commotion of Christ passing by. When he was contemplating the subject, Spencer saw some builders men walk past 'The Nest' with ladders, which for him 'was one part of the "fact" of Christ carrying the Cross. Also my feeling – as is the case always when one comes to wanting to express something – was one of joy. It was joy and all the common everyday occurrences in the village were reassuring, comforting occurrences of that joy . . . The men carried the ladders and Christ carried the Cross' (733.10.58).

As with the companion picture of 'Christ's Entry to Jerusalem' (Leeds City Art Galleries) the passion scene is enacted in a highly charged atmosphere, one of wonder rather than grief. When the Tate Gallery mistakenly titled the work 'Christ Carrying His Cross', Spencer insisted that he had chosen *not* to stress the 'great suffering aspect of the scene' but rather 'the wonder and joy'. In the same document he writes: 'Suppose the whole scene and happening was being re-enacted in Heaven so that now the scene was some manifestation of Heaven. Suppose that one could take a peep into Heaven at the moment this scene was being re-enacted, and suppose one did not know this but only knew that one was having a momentary glimpse of Heaven'.

The reassuring aspect was in part derived from Spencer's own recollection of how 'as youths we stood in a gate opposite our house and watched the people go by on Sundays and in the evenings'. Amid the commotion, Christ appears quite an insignificant figure. The Virgin is depicted 'sitting or stooping' in the left foreground. Four soldiers accompany Christ, but his disciples (who feature in studies for the picture) are absent from the final composition.

Spencer wrote: 'This "side street" feeling might have been helped from hearing Lord Justice Slesser read aloud what he felt to be the finest example of 'sensational journalese'. Spencer recalled the headline in the *Daily Mail* account of the death of Queen Victoria: 'Women publicly wept, and grown men broke down in side streets'. 'If such master strokes of expression can be achieved by means of vulgar journalism let me be a cheap journalist.'

For the catalogue of the Tate Gallery exhibition in 1955, the artist gave a full account of the genesis of the picture: 'The movement of the way to Calvary passes from the right to the left. Rather the movement of a breaker approaching the shore . . . The Cross as far as its position in the picture is concerned is right enough, but I still think it is a pity that I failed to arrive at the notion I hoped for. I had made several drawing attempts of the Cross and disciples ranged somewhat procession-wise either side of it, some of the soldiers helping in the carrying of the Cross . . . some escorting them'.

The Disrobing of Christ   1922
Oil on wood
359 × 635
Presented by the Contemporary Art Society 1938
N04926

In the entry for this picture in his list of paintings (made in 1937), Spencer deleted the word 'disrobing' and wrote 'undressing' instead. This was perhaps to clarify that in the picture Christ is being 'undressed' of his own clothes before being 'robed'. The painting has continued to be known by its original, if misleading, title.

The Robing of Christ   1922
Oil on wood
352 × 594
Presented by the Contemporary Art Society 1938
N04925

This and the preceding picture were painted as predella panels for 'The Betrayal', 1923 (Ulster Museum, Belfast). To the left of the large canvas Spencer planned to hang 'Washing Peter's Feet' and 'The Last Supper', and on the right 'The Disrobing' and 'The Robing of Christ'. The finished predella panels, however, were too large for the main canvas. Spencer painted them whilst lodging in a

teashop in Petersfield in Hampshire. From there he wrote to Henry Lamb 26 May 1922: 'I am doing a thing now which you will dislike and justly. It belongs to my hosiery department. You will see I had four ideas, two of moments in 'The Last Supper' and two of Christ with the soldiers and they were so consecutive and processional, I had to do them. They came out of their shell so nicely . . .' (Tate Archive Microfiche 11).

The subject is from Matthew 27:27–31: 'Then the soldiers of the governor took Jesus into the common hall, and gathered unto him the whole band of soldiers. And they stripped him, and put on him a scarlet robe . . . And after that they had mocked him, they took the robe off from him, and put his own raiment on him, and led him away to crucify him'. Spencer makes a menacing drama out of the play of costumes, sparing none of the torture of Christ's humiliation.

In the thirties, he wrote that 'The Betrayal' was 'full of the qualities which I know are the only things I have fully felt and meant'. Later, he pointed to this particular period as a time when he felt in danger of losing the conviction of his early work which had an inspired 'state of awareness [which] continued to about 1922–23, when I did 'The Betrayal' . . . But I knew in 1922–23 that I was changing or losing grip or something. I feared I was forsaking the vision, and I was filled with consternation'. (Introduction to Tate Gallery exhibition catalogue, 1955.)

The Sword of the Lord and of Gideon   1922–23
Oil on paper
622 × 559
Presented by the Contemporary Art Society 1942
N05321

Spencer wrote of this work: 'A thing I struggled over a great deal. The rocks behind which the soldiers stood should have been on the edge of a road and on the inner of the other side of the road there should have been a rising cliff or hill escarpment. There was something very good there but I could not get at it' (733.3.1).

The biblical narrative is from Judges 7:19–20: 'So Gideon, and the hundred men that were with him, came unto the outside of the camp, in the beginning of the middle watch; . . . and the three companies blew the trumpets, and brake the pitchers, and held the lamps in their left hands, and the trumpets in their right hands to blew withal: and they cried, The Sword of the Lord and of Gideon. And they stood every man in his place round about the camp: and all the host ran, and cried, and fled'.

The chaos of battle (within Spencer's own recent exper-

ience) is rendered in a confusing composition, in which a tent collapses on the soldiers sleeping in blankets beneath. It continues his pre-war interest in Old Testament subjects, the only one such in the group of religious narratives begun in 1920. An earlier date of 1921 has been proposed by Wilenski (p21), Carline (p128) and Bell (p78), supported by Spencer's 1937 list of paintings.

Camouflaged Grenadier   1922–23 (not in display)
Verso: Two Composition Studies for Burghclere Chapel
Pencil and wash on paper
505 × 371
Purchased 1927
N04245

When Spencer returned from the war, he intended to do a series of pictures for a War Memorial. Muirhead Bone's proposals in 1919 for commemorative murals to be painted in his Gloucestershire village of Steep, came to nothing. By 1924, Spencer's ideas had developed into an ambitious scheme when, fortuitously, he found a patron to help realise it. His friend Henry Lamb showed his drawings to Mr and Mrs J L Behrend, (who had already shown interest in his work by buying 'Swan Upping at Cookham' 1915–19), and they decided to build a Chapel to house the scheme. It was to be a memorial to Mrs Behrend's brother, who had died of illness contracted during active service in Macedonia. Spencer's drawings of his own experience of the fighting in Macedonia therefore

made an appropriate memorial. The building was erected in the Behrend's village of Burghclere, in Hampshire. It was designed by Lionel Pearson, working to strict instructions from the artist, and was dedicated as the Oratory of All Souls on 25 March 1927.

Although he had originally hoped to paint the scheme in fresco, in emulation of the Italian masters of the Renaissance, this proved too difficult, and all the panels were painted on canvas. Spencer moved with his family to Burghclere, working there until its completion in 1932.

This is a final study for a soldier coming out of a dugout, camouflaged in ferns. He appears in the foregrouund of the fourth arched-top painting on the north wall of the Chapel, overlooking the altar. Spencer knew the man, a particularly brave character, killed in the fighting in Macedonia.

The Roundabout   1923
Oil on canvas
521 × 457
Presented by the Trustees of the Chantrey Bequest 1944
N05556

Painted in Hampstead, when the artist was working in Henry Lamb's studio on the top floor of the Vale Hotel. The studio windows overlooked the fairground, and Spencer used his unusual vantage point to make a formally arresting composition.

This may be an instance of Spencer trying to produce a more commercially appealing work, perhaps to improve his prospects of marrying Hilda. In any case, it shows how Spencer could be visually, if not imaginatively engaged by the strangeness of an abandoned fairground ride.

The Resurrection, Cookham   1923–27
Oil on canvas
2743 × 5486
Presented by Lord Duveen 1927
N04239 (p40 and 41)

In later years, Spencer looked back on this picture as an example of how he was able to harness a complexity of ideas and feelings in a grand scheme of work: subsequently he wanted but 'never got a comprehensive "setting" a framework such as I found in the subject of the Resurrec-

tion which held me firmly while I viewed the world. I wanted to see all these things through eyes such as that subject gave me' (733.3.22).

At nine feet high and eighteen feet long, 'The Resurrection, Cookham' was by far the largest and most ambitious composition in his career to date. It also marked a turning point in his life, for during the two year gestation of the picture he married Hilda Carline.

It was painted in Henry Lamb's studio in The Vale Hotel, Hampstead, occupying the full length of the room. Spencer stood on boxes to reach the upper sections. The subject he had painted several times before: first in a composition overpainted by 'Apple Gatherers', 1912–13, then in a diptych of 'The Resurrection of the Good and the Bad', 1915, intended for either side of the chancel arch in Cookham Church. At the Slessers' house in 1920 he produced his first sketches for this picture. A phrase of John Donne's description of a churchyard as being 'the holy suburb of Heaven' gave Spencer the idea of setting the Resurrection in Cookham Churchyard.

On the right, ranged alongside the church wall, are venerable 'thinkers' (including Moses) coming back to life in the heat of the sun. A man and his wife emerge reading notes, another man climbs from the grave with a clump of sunflowers on his back. In this section of the picture Spencer includes portraits of his friends and family. Lord Justice Slesser (in his wig) looks suitably lordly as he rises imperiously in a patch of more exotic blooms. Spencer himself is depicted several times, most conspicuously nude, leaning back on a gravestone, facing right. Richard Carline, his friend and then brother-in-law, kneels naked, facing left. At the lower right of the picture Spencer appears again, reclining in an open tomb, in the 'state of rest and contentment' which pervades the scene. 'The open book and my resting on it is the shape of my soul', his 'signature' he later called it.

On the left, Hilda makes repeated appearances just as Stanley does on the right. She appears reclining on the ivy-covered tomb in the foreground, and smelling a flower on the path. Through the dry caked earth a group of black people emerge, signifying that all cultures and creeds are part of this spiritual regeneration. Spencer gives his river scene an Arcadian glow, a landscape passage which he was later to admire.

Of the central section, Spencer later asked the question: 'what's all that under the porch? Once again everything was clear except the chiefest and most important thing and once again I was robbed of that special privilege of succeeding where success is vital and must be' (733.3.22). In the porch, God the Father stands behind a maternal looking Christ (cradling children and a diminutive naked man). Spencer had Hilda pose for both figures and he was much preoccupied at the time in coming to terms with this relationship, which was consummated in marriage on 23 February 1925. Spencer forever attempted to integrate his sexual union with Hilda with his spiritual identity. 'I can see how my marriage experience from 1923 to the present day has affected my work. I wished and hoped that my first marriage would form part of my religious outlook'. In this painting at least, he was able to enthrone his happiness and joy with Hilda in a vision which redeemed his earlier sexual and artistic frustrations.

When John Rothenstein visited Spencer in his Hampstead studio, the Resurrection was leaning against the wall: 'The room was barely large enough to accommodate the immense canvas, which leaned against the longest wall. Up against the canvas stood a small table – which, with two kitchen chairs and a small tin bath was the room's only furniture – and upon it a large teapot, half a dozen unwashed plates and some white marmalade jars, some containing paintbrushes and others marmalade. (Rothenstein, 1984, p95). The 'perpetual steaming kettle' was later to be blamed for an area of paint instability in the canvas.

Rothenstein's judgement of the picture was that although it is 'a summing up of the artist's past achievement, it has one characteristic that marks it as belonging to the later period of Spencer's growth when his art had lost its God-centred simplicity and had become comprehensive. This picture is full of beauties, full even of splendours. It seems to me to be one of the great pictures of this century. Yet, in comparison with the best of the artist's earlier works, it is over-crowded, loosely composed, imperfectly focused' (Rothenstein, p109).

The picture was the centre of attention at Spencer's first exhibition at the Goupil Gallery in spring 1927, and made him a public figure. *The Times* (28 February 1927) called it 'the most important picture painted by any English artist in the present century . . . What makes it so astonishing is the combination in it of careful detail with modern freedom of form. It is as if a Pre-Raphaelite had shaken hands with a Cubist'. The Bloomsbury critic, Roger Fry, gave qualified praise: 'Mr Spencer is a literary painter, he works by imagery. Our quarrel with such should not be that they are plastic . . . but that, for the most part, their imagery is so dull and inexpressive. That complaint cannot be levelled against 'The Resurrection'. It is highly arresting and intriguing. It is no perfunctory sentimental piece of story-telling, but a very personal conception carried through with unfailing nerve and conviction' (*National and Athenaeum*, 12 March 1927).

'The Resurrection, Cookham' was bought by Lord Duveen from the exhibition for £1,000, for presentation to the National Collection.

Turkeys 1925
Oil on canvas
508 × 762
Presented by the Contemporary Art Society 1935
N04800

In 1951, Spencer dated this picture to 1925, the year of his marriage to Hilda. It was probably painted in the Suffolk village of Wangford, where Hilda had been a land-girl during the war, and where they married on 23 February 1925.

Spencer uses the skeletal structure of the shed to make bold play of interconnecting verticals and horizontals between it, the fence slats, and gate.

Tree and Chicken Coops, Wangford 1925
Oil on canvas
457 × 762
Bequeathed by Sir Edward Marsh through the Contemporary Art Society 1953
N06150

Painted during Spencer's first year of marriage. He was later to return to Wangford after the collapse of his second

The Resurrection, Cookham 1923–27 (p38)

marriage to Patricia Preece.

Although painted 'en plein air', the composition shows some effort on the artist's part to produce a serious and saleable landscape in the Dutch tradition. It is in keeping with his affection for domestic matters (whether human or animal) that he should choose to include the chicken coops, as outdoor habitations. The artist said that he had in mind Scottish ballads such as 'The Twa Corbies'.

us . . . I thought how extraordinary she looked. I felt sure she had the same mental attitude towards things as I had. I could feel my true self in that extraordinary person . . .' (Rothenstein, 1979, p24).

This drawing (also known as 'Hilda with hair down') is one of several studies from this period, including 'Hilda with Beads' (below). As he frequently did, Spencer here enlarged the drawing with the addition of a second, larger sheet.

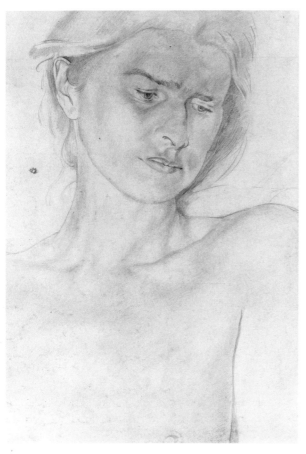

Portrait of Hilda   1931
Pencil on paper
788 × 628
Lent by Mrs Richard Carline, the artist's sister-in-law
1984
L00629

Hilda with Beads   1931
Pencil on paper
692 × 546
Private Collection, Liverpool

A study of Hilda, made at Burghclere, where they lived whilst Stanley worked on the Chapel. Hilda Carline was a painter, from an artistic Hampstead family, and an independent woman with strong views of her own. Spencer met her through her brother Sydney Carline, another Slade student. 'As she came toward me . . . and the rest of

Spencer used this drawing as the basis of a later oil painting of Hilda, 'Seated Nude', completed in 1942, (private collection) some six years after their separation. He mentions both the drawing and painting in a letter to her dated 13 May 1937: 'About six months ago I did an oil painting of you from that nude to the waist drawing I did of you at Burghclere. Even that is extraordinary next to the ones of Patricia. I think that even while now we are in the midst of this legal fight that in our real selves we continue to be utterly at one, rejoicing in our oneness' (733.3.31).

The oil was his only nude painting of Hilda. Spencer included the painting in his list of nudes (p21), and wrote that he wished to make a series of nudes of Hilda, as he had done of Patricia.

Turk's Boatyard, Cookham   c1931
Oil on canvas
635 × 765
Bequeathed by Mrs I M Andrews 1970
T01207 (p11)

Turk's Boatyard features in 'Swan Upping at Cookham' (p13). Spencer's affection for the fabric of village life was centred on the river activity, and Cookham Bridge. The artist frames his composition from a standing height, looking down on the punts, directing the viewer's attention to the ground – a favourite device in his landscape paintings.

In an undated letter to the original owner of the picture, Mrs Andrews, written at Burghclere, Spencer wrote that the purchase came at an opportune time, when he had to meet the expenses of a recent operation, and the purchase of a house, 'Lindworth'.

Terry's Lane, Cookham   c1932
Oil on canvas
508 × 762
Purchased 1933
N04678 (p17)

Gilbert Spencer recalled that Terry's Lane was a favourite childhood walk of his brother and himself, by which they reached the railway bridge. Spencer knits the three bushes into the landscape behind, creating a disquieting sense of fusion within the picture, despite the ordinariness of the motif. Dudley Tooth, who from 1932 was the artist's sole dealer, encouraged the production of landscapes for the market. Spencer later dated this work to about 1932, the year he was elected Associate of the Royal Academy, and invited to show ten works in the British Pavilion of the Venice Biennale.

St Francis and the Birds   1935
Oil on canvas
660 × 584
Presented by the Trustees of the Chantrey Bequest 1967
T00961

'Eleven days before the day for sending to the Academy I began the St Francis and the birds picture, which is nearly the smallest figure picture I have ever painted. The figure of St Francis stands *facing* the spectator and turns his head sharply over to the spectators left and gazes upwards' (733.2.32).

Spencer traced the origins of this picture to a drawing of 1924 showing Hilda lying reading on a haystack, surrounded by a flock of chickens and ducks (used in the Chatto and Windus *Almanac* of 1927). 'As so often happened when I have attempted to do this most difficult kind of artistic endeavour, the idea for this picture did not come to me all at once and these interruptions and headings off have finally made it necessary for me to attempt a fusion of the parts. For seventeen years or more I have possessed St Francis books *The Little Flowers of St Francis* and *The Mirror of Perfection*, and I am well acquainted with their contents'. Of this picture he wrote: 'In this preaching to the birds I conceive that St Francis is expressing also his union with nature and the romantic wilderness of it as being expressed in him almost more than it is in the birds many of which are consequently domestic. The shapes and forms of St Francis are contiguously considered with the surrounding shapes and forms which further intensifies the union between them' (733.2.45).

Spencer later told the compiler of the Tate Gallery catalogue that 'the figure of St Francis is large and spreading to signify that the teaching of St Francis spread far and wide'. He also told his biographer Maurice Collis that St Francis 'was imagined by the memory of his father in a dressing gown going to the larder in the passage between 'Fernlea' and 'The Nest' to get food for the hens and ducks. His trousers were at one time stolen and he went about the village for a bit in his dressing gown'.

The picture caused a furore when, together with 'The Dustman' (or 'Lovers') of 1934, it was rejected by the hanging committee of the Royal Academy for their Summer Exhibition. Spencer was affronted and resigned as an ARA. The incident prompted letters in the press, most of them ridiculing the painting as a caricature, but the artist C R W Nevinson was quoted as saying that 'Mr Spencer is far too good a painter to belong to the Royal Academy'. In 1950 Spencer was persuaded to rejoin the Academy, prompting a *News Review* magazine article entitled 'The Return of A Rebel'.

Nude, Portrait of Patricia Preece   1935
Oil on canvas
508 × 762
Ivor Braka Limited, London (p22)

This is one of Spencer's earliest nude paintings of Patricia, and the first to portray her in a reclining position. Later he would use the pose in the two double nudes of 1936 and 1937. It was painted at 'Lindworth' from life, and is one of his most startlingly direct compositions. The contorted nature of their relationship, which Stanley was struggling to formalise, is here given memorable expression. 'I have never used professional models', he wrote, 'not liking the idea'. Like an ant crawling over the flesh (Spencer's own phrase), the artist's eye charts the topography of Patricia's naked body as alien territory. The head, squeezed into the upper corner, becomes dislocated from the body, and is made to compete with the breasts as the focus of attention. By folding the body, and realigning it on the horizontal, he manages to defamiliarise it. Spencer, it would seem, relished the challenge of compressing the full figure into what was his standard size canvas of 30 × 20 inches.

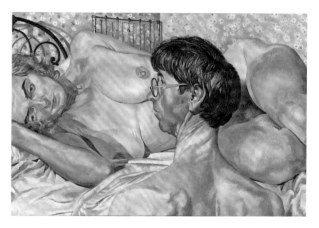

Self-Portrait with Patricia Preece   1936
610 × 914
Oil on canvas
Lent by the Syndics of the Fitzwilliam Museum, Cambridge

This is the first of the two double nudes which Spencer painted of himself and Patricia. It is only slightly larger than the 30 × 20 canvas on which he painted the reclining 'Nude, Portrait of Patricia Preece' (p22) the previous year. Here, she lies more naturally on the bed, her body seen squarely in the middle of the picture, her legs severely foreshortened. Stanley's head looms in front of her belly, occupying the area between her breasts and her crotch. The bleached skin of his neck and back blends with the sheets, making his head seem even more of a detached presence. Colour is carefully orchestrated: Stanley's cheeks, flushed with excitement, pick up the pigments of her lips and nipples, as if he paints himself into her body, in a futile attempt at oneness. His use of black creates a starker effect, linking Stanley's full head of hair with Patricia's arched eyebrows and the iron bedstead behind, which seems to reinforce her unyielding position.

Despite the apparent proximity of their bodies, it is the emotional and psychological disconnection between them which gives the composition its dramatic force. By comparison with the later 'Double Nude Portrait' (right), this is the more straightforward and hence affecting account of misplaced tenderness and carnal desire.

Double Nude Portrait: The Artist and his Second Wife 1937
Oil on canvas
838 × 937
Purchased 1974
T01863

Painted at 'Lindworth', this is the second, and more icono-
graphically complex of the two double nudes. It was
referred to by Spencer variously as 'Double Nude and
Stove' and 'the big double nude'. In a note written the
following year, he records: 'I also began . . . a painting in
the evening from life of a double nude. A man sits and
contemplates the woman. He is squatting and fills the
space between the woman's arms resting above her head
and her raised knees . . . Both figures are life-size – The
uncooked supper is in the foreground and on the right is a
Valor oil stove lit' (733.2.34).

Although providing a prosaic explanation of the meat
and the stove, in giving them prominence in the composition Spencer undoubtedly invested the various elements
with some meaning. The uneaten flesh is an inescapable
reference to their unconsummated relationship, and the
burning heat of the stove a further analogy to stoked, if
forcibly contained, passion.

Certainly Spencer thought contemptible what he saw as
the prudishness of the Church's attitude to sexuality, and
felt strongly enough about its centrality to human existence to express his ideas at some length, in writing and in
painting. Spencer planned in his Church-House scheme to
have a room given over to display the nudes, which
'would show how much they balance a need in the whole
cosmic conception . . . I wanted in the nude section to

show the analogy between the Church and the prescribed
nature of worship, and human love'. His head bent
solemnly over her body betokens a ritual act of worship:
sex as sacrament, contemplated but not partaken. Patricia's splayed body belies her unavailing refusal to sacrifice
anything of herself.

In later years Spencer could still be surprised and
impressed by the picture. In September 1955 he wrote: 'I
have now brought back home the big double nude. When
I put it alongside any other of my work it shows how
needed it is to give my work the variety that is so refresh-
ing. This big double nude is rather a remarkable thing.
There is in it male, female and animal flesh. The remarkable thing is that to me it is absorbing and restful to look
at. There is none of my usual imagination in this thing: it
is direct from nature and my imagination never works
faced with objects or landscape. But there is something
satisfying in looking at it. It was done with zest and my
direct painting capacity I had'.

'I feel all the time how much my shows need these
nudes. I shall have to start on myself only it is very tiring.
And I don't want to be hurried' (733.8.2).

Rickett's Farm, Cookham Dene 1938
Oil on canvas
660 × 1168
Purchased 1938
N04942

Cookham Dene was a small hamlet just outside Cookham
village. It is possible to see in Spencer's choice of subject
his preoccupation with the inside brought outside. The
paint-peeled doors of suburban homes now house the
families of pigs. Such makeshift homeliness may have had
some poignancy for Spencer in 1938. His marriage, just

45

one year previously, to Patricia Preece had proved to be an abject failure. In 1938, she proposed to sell 'Lindworth', forcing his move from Cookham to the shelter of friends in London. The domestic order he painstakingly observes outdoors was sadly lacking in his own affairs.

Daphne   1940
Oil on canvas
610 × 508
Purchased 1940
N05148

Daphne Charlton was a Slade-trained artist, whose husband George taught at the college. They were introduced to Spencer in the summer of 1939 by the artist C R W Nevinson, Stanley's friend from student days. Stanley shared with Daphne his love of music, and he often visited their home in New End Square, Hampstead. In the summer of 1939, they invited Spencer to join them for a painting holiday in Gloucestershire, staying at the White Hart Inn, Leonard Stanley.

Daphne sat for the portrait every day for about two to three weeks in April 1940. The hat she wears was bought for three guineas in Bond Street in December 1939, especially for the sittings. Another portrait of Daphne shows her without her hat. Their relationship revived Spencer's craving for intimacy, and fed his capacity for

sexual fantasy. 'Our bedroom love was taken up Gypsy Lane and over the stiles and across the meadows and along the roads back up to our room. Then after more love in the bedroom, we went out among the elm trees and cattle and chickens, and were conscious and did as we had just done in bed, so that our private life was public. I liked having trees and grass and puddles and chickens and the sun in the same association as bedclothes' (annotations on reverse of 'The Tiger Rug' study, quoted in Pople, p409).

Spencer described Daphne in a letter to Hilda as 'in certain ways being quite sophisticated, but I have found certain things in her which are touching. She is a restless, turbulent spirit' (733.3.1, also 733.4.3). This portrait, with its domestic interior, and the suffocating attention to the pattern and textures of fabrics and hair, is charged with an erotic excitement, registered in the sitter's pursed red lips.

Spencer recalled visiting an exhibition of recent purchases by the Tate Gallery 'and my portrait of Daphne in a black hat was there as also was the Daphne herself in the hat getting quite a bit of "glory" out of it all. It's pathetic that her portrait of me done when at Leonard Stanley was rejected by the R.A.' (733.2.63).

Spencer's attachment to the Port Glasgow shipyard workers and their families, in whose company he had been able to work productively, was celebrated in the great series of paintings he made between 1945 and 1950. He wrote in his notebooks 'I soon found that the shipyard at Port Glasgow is only one aspect of the life there. There were rows of men and women hurrying in the streets, and high sunlit factory walls with men sitting or standing or leaning back against them, and early shoppers going to and fro; one day through the crack of a factory door I glimpsed a cascade of brass tap; in a roadway (a very trafficky one) I saw children lying on the ground using the road as their drawing board and making drawings in coloured chalk; and there was a long seat on which old men sat removed from the passers-by like statues . . . all this . . . seemed to me full of some inward surging meaning, a kind of joy, that I longed to get closer to and understand and in some way fulfill' (Rothenstein, 1984, p119). Spencer described how there was 'an undefined not-yet-come-to-earth Port Glasgow epitomising something I hope to find and arrive at . . . I kept wondering what form it can have and . . . what could realise all that meaning that keeps peeping at me from all and everything happening here'. He recalled how, unable to sleep one night, he went for a walk down by the gas-works, and came across the cemetery, which to Spencer, seemed the spiritual heart of the town. 'I felt that all this life and meaning somehow grouped round and in some way led up to the cemetery on the hill outside the town, an oval saucer-upside-down-shaped hill of green mound in a nest of red . . . And I began to see the Port Glasgow Resurrection that I have drawn and painted in the last five years. As it has worked out this hillside cemetery has become The Hill of Sion' (Rothenstein, 1984, p119). The hill of the graveyard looked to the artist like 'what the Arabian Nights call the mountain of the bereft' although in his vision it was to 'become the hill of the blessed' (733.8.61).

Spencer planned one huge canvas, some fifty feet across, but in the end settled to the more practical solution of a number of independent, interrelated paintings. 'The Resurrection: Port Glasgow', 1947–50 is only one of two in the series made to the scale of his original plans. It was originally two-thirds the present size, until Spencer added the 'table tomb' scene, shifting the focus, and then added a further nine feet of canvas to balance the whole picture.

Describing the painting, Spencer divided it into three sections: the central section of men and women who are '(such is my intention) feeling happy as they read the references made to themselves on the tomb lid', while children 'scramble about'. The grandparents in the foreground 'have crawled from their respective graves towards each other; they are passionately happy to see each other and look steadfastly and with wonder at each other'. In them, Spencer wanted 'to suggest something of the growing together from the two worlds of a long married couple the togetherness and yet separateness, and also something of the mystery of the resurrection, the meeting of two worlds, this world and the resurrected-life world' (Wilenski, 1951, p8).

Drawing for left-hand section of *Resurrection: Reunion*
Pencil on paper
403 × 267
Purchased 1980
T03045

A finished drawing, of c1945, for 'The Resurrection: Reunion', 1945 (Aberdeen City Art Gallery and Museum), showing the reunion of families after the resurrection. Spencer delights in the horizontal arrangement of the cast-iron railings which he had seen in the Port Glasgow cemetery. In the foreground a husband leans over his newly resurrected wife, their hands raised in wonder and amazement, as a child clambers onto the mother's lap. Others behind them limber up and stretch themselves. Spencer described how the group of children 'squat by and hold on to the railing as they might of their own garden [fence] or crib', while 'a wife uses her husband's outstretched leg as a safe fence for looking into the beyond'. Nearby a 'still living mother' is reunited with her resurrected child.

'Here I had the feeling that each grave forms part of a person's home just as their front gardens do, so that a row of graves and a row of cottage gardens have much the same meaning for me. Also although the people are adult or any age, I think of them in cribs or prams or mangers. *Grown-ups in prams* would perhaps express what I was after – the sense of security and peace that a babe has as it gazes over the rim of its pram out into the world around it.'

In the painting, the naked figure is clothed.

Drawing for right-hand section of *Resurrection: Reunion*
Pencil on paper
403 × 267
Purchased 1980
T03047

A drawing for 'The Resurrection: Reunion', 1945. Spencer described the difference between the 'Reunion' composition and the earlier 'Port Glasgow Resurrection' in commentaries written for R W Wilenski's book on the series, published in 1951. 'In the large 'Resurrection' picture there are some still living people (the mourners) as well as the risen dead. In 'Reunion' this is carried further and I have tried to suggest the circumstances of the resurrection through the quick and the dead, between the visitors to a cemetery and the dead now rising from it. These visitors are in the central panel, and the resurrected are in the panels right and left. In the foreground of the right panel is a heart-shaped tombstone, behind which a couple embrace affectionately, watched by two adoring women. In the middle a resurrected woman leans back against a stone, propped by an iron stand, using it as a chair back; she greets her resurrected children who climb from out of the ground into her lap and arms. In the row above this there are three graves. Their headstones are held by each resurrected one as they might a large photograph frame . . . In this panel I liked and wanted the feeling that it was all just meadowlands and also somehow like heaven and I have tried to get this ordinary and-yet-not-ordinary-land feel of a place where whatever happened would be of a different order of happening from what took place on the cemetery drive in the centre.'

Drawing for right-hand section of *Resurrection: Port Glasgow*
Pencil on paper
403 × 267
Purchased 1980
T03042

Drawing for part of the right-hand section of *Resurrection: Port Glasgow*
Pencil on paper
403 × 267
Purchased 1980
T03039

A drawing for 'The Resurrection: Port Glasgow', 1947–50, showing a young girl being helped from her grave by a man who offers his back as a step, watched by the 'gravedigger who calmly surveys the whole scene'.

Spencer used only a modified version of this drawing for the right-hand section of 'The Resurrection: Port Glasgow'. A woman lies on her tomb, hands raised as though in levitation. Her visitors beckon to others to come to witness the moment of resurrection. A young girl, fallen asleep while watching, is yet unaware of the startling event. The resurrected woman does not appear in the painting.

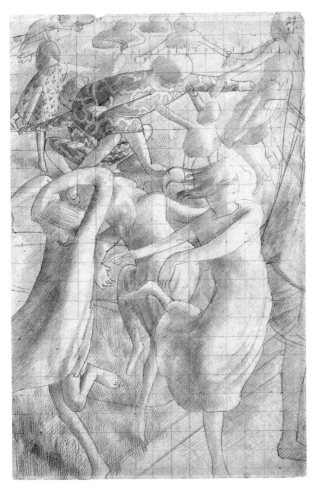

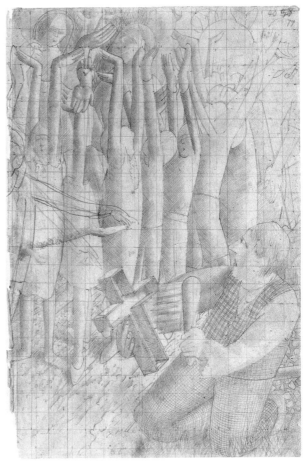

Drawing for the left-hand section of *Resurrection: Rejoicing*
Pencil on paper
403 × 267
Purchased 1980
T03036

Drawing for the central section of *Resurrection: Rejoicing*
Pencil on paper
403 × 267
Purchased 1980
T03037

A drawing for 'The Resurrection: Rejoicing', 1947, (The Beaverbrook Art Gallery Fredericton, New Brunswick). Spencer uses cross-hatching to build up the basic forms of the dancing women and children, omitting the detail of the flowers and the gravel path, and all but two of the patterns on the dresses. In the background the resurrected link arms and encourage the women leaning over the hedge to join in the celebrations.

A squared-up drawing of 1944 for the central section of 'Resurrection: Rejoicing', 1947. It depicts the joyful resurrection 'of the quick and the dead', which is witnessed as a kind of vision by the people tending graves. Spencer wrote, 'the children raise their arms in ecstasy. Behind them grown-up women look after them or join them in their joy. In the foreground portion a man brushes out a cross-shaped flower trough'.

Here a group of children, with women behind, perform an unrestrained jazz-like dance of joy, to the amazement of the man dusting out a cross-shaped 'flower trough'.

The tubular figure style recalls that of William Roberts in the twenties.

Drawing for the left-hand section of *Resurrection: Waking Up*
Pencil on paper
403 × 267
Purchased 1980
T03043

This drawing is one of a number of studies which Spencer made for 'Resurrection: Waking Up', 1945, (The Nevill Gallery, Canterbury and Bath). The artist described how, in 'the pencil composition of the right hand panel I had two kitchen alarum clocks rolling in the grass. Although there is no likelihood of such things being in a graveyard, I think it was a mistake not to have kept them in the painting'. Here, some women yawn and stretch and rub their eyes, while children crawl around a gravestone.

Drawing for the left-hand section of *Resurrection: Reunion of Families, Mother and Children*
Pencil on paper
403 × 267
Purchased 1980
T03050

A drawing for the left-hand section of 'The Resurrection: Reunion of Families', 1945, (Birmingham Museum and Art Gallery). A mother turns and leans on her gravestone to see her children, the eldest of whom stretches out her hand to touch the woman's face. Others come up behind carrying flowers arranged under glass, whilst to the right, a man greets his newly resurrected wife.

Dinner on the Hotel Lawn 1956–57
Oil on canvas
949 × 1359
Presented by the Trustees of the Chantrey Bequest 1957
T00141

Self Portrait 1959
Oil on canvas
508 × 406
Presented by the Friends of the Tate Gallery 1982
T03335

In 1952 Spencer began a series of pictures on 'Christ Preaching at Cookham Regatta', drawing on his childhood memories of the event. In this, the fourth, a grand reception takes place on the lawns of the Ferry Hotel, by the banks of the Thames. Christ is preaching from the horse-ferry barge moored up river, out of view. Some commotion attends the serving of dinner. Spencer remarked that he only used these long tables in this picture, the others being square. 'In all of them I seem to have forgotten about the food, square or long table. And I was annoyed to notice that I had made the servants putting the knives on the wrong side of the table: and they are doing it so nicely' (Tate Gallery Catalogue, p672).

In an earlier study for this composition, Spencer intended to have Christ moored in the landing in the background, with the disciples moving among the guests. The red-haired woman on the four-legged stool who extends her reach across (and off) the table is one of Spencer's more bizarre creations.

This is the artist's penultimate picture. A typewritten label on the back of the canvas reads: 'Self-portrait by STANLEY SPENCER / Sunday July 12 to / Thursday July 16th 1959 / Painted in the drawing room / Hill Head House / Dewsbury / Yorkshire'. The note is initialled by Mrs Joy Fothergill Smith, with whom he was staying. In December 1958 the artist had been diagnosed as suffering from cancer, and had undergone a colostomy operation.

Spencer stayed with Mrs Smith and her family for a fortnight, buying the canvas for this picture in an artists' materials shop in Leeds. He first of all made a red conte-crayon drawing similar in size to the painting, using a looking glass brought downstairs from his bedroom. The picture was worked from the eyes outwards.

The patterned wallpaper and picture jutting out behind his head, create an optical tension demanding greater effort of concentration on the face. In a frontal composition, everything is shifting and askew. The strain of terminal illness is kept at bay by the candour of his gaze.

In remarks made to students at Ruskin School of Drawing at Oxford in 1922 Spencer had said: 'The first place an artist should find himself is in prison. The moment he realises he is a prisoner, he is an artist, and the moment he is an artist, he starts to free himself'.